The Best
Stage Scenes
of 2008

Edited and with a Foreword
by Lawrence Harbison

SCENE STUDY SERIES

A SMITH AND KRAUS BOOK

Published by Smith and Kraus, Inc.
177 Lyme Road, Hanover, NH 03755
SmithandKraus.com

First Edition: February 2009
10 9 8 7 6 5 4 3 2 1
Cover illustration by Lisa Goldfinger
Cover and text design by Julia Hill Gignoux,
Freedom Hill Design and Book Production

The Scene Study Series 1067-3253
ISBN-13 978-1-57525-621-4 / ISBN-10 1-57525-621-5
Library of Congress Control Number: 2008941389

**NOTE: These scenes are intended to be used for audition and class study; permission
is not required to use the material for those purposes. However, if there is a paid performance of any of the scenes included in this book, please refer to the Rights and
Permissions pages 217–218 to locate the source that can grant permission for public
performance.**

To receive prepublication information about upcoming Smith and Kraus books and information about special promotions, send us your e-mail address at info@smithandkraus.com with
a subject line of MAILING LIST. *Call toll-free (888) 282-2881 or visit us at SmithandKraus.com.*

CONTENTS

SCENES FOR TWO WOMEN

Foreword

In these pages you will find a rich and varied selection of scenes from recent plays, for a wide variety of age groups. Many are comic (laughs), many are dramatic (generally, no laughs). Some are rather short, some are rather long. All represent the best in contemporary playwriting.

Several of these pieces are by playwrights whose work may be familiar to you such as Don Nigro, Theresa Rebeck, Adam Bock, José Rivera, Peter Parnell and Aaron Sorkin; others are by exciting up-and-comers like Jim Knabel, Hilary Bettis, Rogelio Martinez, Mike Batistick, Catherine Trieschmann, Anne Garcia-Romero, Jenny Lyn Bader and David Davalos. All are representative of the best of contemporary writing for the stage.

Most of the plays from which these scenes have been culled have been published and, hence, are readily available either from the publisher/licensor or from a theatrical book store such as Drama Book Shop in New York. A few plays may not be published for a while, in which case contact the author or his agent for a copy of the entire text of the play which suits your fancy. Information on publishers/rights holders may be found in the Rights and Permissions section in the back of this anthology.

Break a leg in that audition! Knock 'em dead in class!

Lawrence Harbison
Brooklyn, NY

SCENES FOR ONE MAN AND ONE WOMAN

ALL EYES AND EARS

Rogelio Martinez

Dramatic
Carmen and Alvaro, thirties

> *It is 1961 in Havana and Carmen works as an informer for the government. Here she and her husband discuss whether or not to inform on someone they know.*

ALVARO: Carmen. Do you think he knows more than he's shared with you?

CARMEN: *(Shaking her head no.)* I don't know.

ALVARO: That's better. This is a good place to begin.

(Beat.)

ALVARO: *(Continued.)* I want to inform you that his friend Flores with the American cigarettes — we picked up some letter that were intended for him.

CARMEN: He's not really friends with Flores.

ALVARO: They sometimes shoot pool together.

CARMEN: Sometimes but —

ALVARO: Flores's nephew worked for the Richard Nixon Election Committee in South Florida.

CARMEN: I don't know what that is.

ALVARO: I hope that when the time comes I can trust you to do the right thing.

(Alvaro starts to lead Carmen out.)

ALVARO: *(Continued.)* Let me ask you one more thing. You knew about his skipping Sundays. Not showing up for volunteer work. You knew he was doing that. Why didn't you put that information in any of your reports?

(Beat.)

CARMEN: No.

ALVARO: What?

CARMEN: I didn't know.

   (Beat.)

ALVARO: Stepan, may I have a moment with . . .

   (Stepan exits.)

ALVARO: *(Continued.)* I'm sorry, he seems to be keeping secrets from both of us. I'm sorry that you're the last one to find out. Would you like a glass of water.

   (She shakes her head no.)

   Can I get you anything? Sit down. Carmen. Are you all right?

CARMEN: She may be involved.

ALVARO: Who?

CARMEN: My husband's ex-wife. She may be involved in the whole thing. For all I know it's her. It's probably just her. I know my husband has nothing to do with it. I know it's her. And if he's skipping Sundays is because he's trying to stop her from being involved against this government.

ALVARO: Slow down. I need a name.

CARMEN: Josefina Lourdes Vega. Before I met my husband he was married to her — briefly. She's never been able to get over the divorce. When we moved to this new house I thought we would be far enough from her — she lives on the other side of town. There we used to run into her quite a lot but I don't see her anymore. He still sees her. He still visits her. She's involved.

ALVARO: Involved in what?

CARMEN: She has family in Santa Clara. Some of her family was part of the Batista government. I believe she's involved with them — with trying to stop the change that's happening.

ALVARO: But you don't know for sure.

CARMEN: I do. I do know for sure. I haven't put it in the reports but — well she has . . . she has . . . her family is in Florida. She has told people in the neighborhood that in Florida every house has air conditioner and that the power does not go out at night and that cars . . . there are highways and there's always milk . . . and it's not powdered unless you're poor. And then one time she said, We're all poor here we just don't know it because we have no one different around us to compare ourselves to.

(Alvaro stops writing.)

ALVARO: Not enough.

CARMEN: What?

ALVARO: There's not enough there.

CARMEN: She is involved.

ALVARO: I don't believe you.

CARMEN: I didn't make those things up.

ALVARO: I don't think you made them up. I believe those are things your husband has said.

CARMEN: No.

ALVARO: Yes.

CARMEN: Yes.
> *(Pause.)*

ALVARO: Can I ask you something, Carmen? Something perhaps — I want to ask you something personal.

CARMEN: What?

ALVARO: When did you and your husband last have intimate relations?
> *(She cries. It's subtle.)*
> *(Pause.)*

ALVARO: *(Continued.)* May I have the book? The report I asked you to read.
> *(She removes it from her purse.)*

ALVARO: You have told me what's happening in everyone's bedroom. Now I want you to tell me what's happening in yours.
> *(Beat.)*

CARMEN: Nothing.
> *(She gives him the book.)*

ALVARO: We've known about the affair. I'm sorry this is the way you had to find out.
> *(Alvaro reaches out to her.)*

CARMEN: I knew. I even told him I knew. I was lying. I didn't know.
> *(She is in his arms now.)*

CARMEN: *(Continued.)* Sometimes I wish this revolution had never happened. Then I could have stayed a little longer in the dark.

DEATHBED
Mark Schultz

Dramatic
Danny and Martha, thirties

> *Martha has been diagnosed with terminal cancer. Her husband, Danny, just can't promise that he will be able to help her deal with it. It's just too much for him.*

DANNY: This is hard for me.
MARTHA: OK.
DANNY: It is.
MARTHA: I know.
DANNY: You don't.
MARTHA: OK.
DANNY: I've tried.
MARTHA: OK.
    (Beat.)
DANNY: I don't like pain.
MARTHA: Who does?
DANNY: I don't like sickness.
MARTHA: Don't blame you.
DANNY: I don't like death.
MARTHA: Great. Yes. I know.
DANNY: And I want to love you more.
MARTHA: Then do it.
DANNY: But I can't.
    (Beat.)
    I'm sorry.
MARTHA: Um.
DANNY: That's all.
MARTHA: Um.
DANNY: OK?

MARTHA: No.

DANNY: Sorry.

MARTHA: Me too.

> *(Beat.)*

DANNY: Don't look at me like that. Martha. Please.

> *(Beat.)*
>
> You can't expect people. Someone. Me. To live with that. You can't expect that from someone. Day in day out. Death. Coming. Around the corner. You can't expect that. That's not life. That's not living. That's not fair. I'm sorry but it's not.
>
> *(Beat.)*
>
> And it's not like I haven't tried. I did try. I tried very hard. Very very hard. I read brochures. I listened to you. Talking. And suffering. I did. All I could. As much as I could.
>
> *(Beat.)*
>
> And I love you. I do. I really do. But I'm sorry. That's just. I'm sorry. I really am. I'm sorry.
>
> *(Beat.)*
>
> And I don't expect. Forgiveness. I don't expect that. But if you could just. Try. And understand. How hard —
>
> *(Beat.)*
>
> Martha you can't look at me like that. You can't. It's not fair.
>
> *(Pause.)*

MARTHA: How should I look at you?

> *(Silence.)*

DANNY: Call me when you're better. We'll work something out.

> *(Danny makes to leave.)*

MARTHA: Don't go. Please. Stay.

DANNY: I can't.

MARTHA: Just a little bit.

DANNY: Found someone else.

MARTHA: It's OK.

DANNY: Someone healthy.

MARTHA: It's fine.

DANNY: Don't say that.

MARTHA: OK.

DANNY: It's not fine.

MARTHA: Can't hate you.

DANNY: Why not?

MARTHA: Because.

DANNY: Better if you do.

MARTHA: I can't. Is all. Stay.

    (Beat.)

DANNY: No.

MARTHA: Just a bit.

DANNY: Can't.

MARTHA: Danny.

DANNY: I can't.

MARTHA: Please.

DANNY: Martha.

MARTHA: Please.

    (Beat.)

    Just a bit.

    (Silence.)

DANNY: Not too long.

    (Danny sits. Martha sits next to him.)

    (Silence.)

    (Martha lays her head in his lap.)

MARTHA: Can I?

DANNY: Um.

MARTHA: Last time.

DANNY: Fine. Sure. For a bit.

    (Beat.)

MARTHA: I used to do this. A long time ago.

DANNY: I know.

MARTHA: And you would hold me.

DANNY: I know.

MARTHA: Tell me you loved me.

DANNY: I would.

    (Beat.)

MARTHA: But now its very late.

DANNY: It is.

MARTHA: And things change.

DANNY: They do.

MARTHA: And nothing is ever as beautiful as it's meant to be.

DANNY: Maybe.

MARTHA: As you remembered it could be.

DANNY: Maybe.

MARTHA: But I've never found. That that was ever any reason. To stop loving something.

(Beat.)

OK?

(Beat. Danny looks at his watch.)

DANNY: I have an hour. Then I have to go.

MARTHA: Thank you.

DANNY: Just an hour.

MARTHA: How generous.

DANNY: That's it.

MARTHA: I'll take what I can get.

THE DRUNKEN CITY
Adam Bock

Seriocomic
Frank and Marnie, twenties

> *Marnie, out on the town with two girlfriends, has just met Frank*
> *— and the two have fallen for each other. Here they are off on their*
> *own and have wandered into a church.*

> *Marnie and Frank enter. They are entering a church. Alone. Sweet,*
> *dim light.*

FRANK: How's this?

MARNIE: Are you sure we should be in here?

FRANK: This is one of the last churches in the city that doesn't lock its doors at night. In case someone's in trouble I figure. We're in trouble right?

MARNIE: I've never been in a church in the middle of the night.

FRANK: I figured you want it quiet.

MARNIE: It's beautiful.

FRANK: Look at the.

MARNIE: Gary would laugh.

FRANK: Why?

MARNIE: I don't like going to church with him. He starts sitting up straight.

FRANK: You wanna get out of here?

MARNIE: No. I like it here with you. Stop it. Don't kiss me!

FRANK: Why not?

MARNIE: It's church!

FRANK: So?

MARNIE: Jesus is right there!

FRANK: He doesn't mind.

MARNIE: Frank be serious.

FRANK: I am. He's up there smiling at us.

MARNIE: I'm not kissing you in a church. I got more important things to figure out. Be serious.

FRANK: You were going to kiss Gary in a church.

MARNIE: You gotta help me figure this out. Please?

FRANK: Why'd you even tell him yes?

MARNIE: I wanted the wedding.

FRANK: What? That's just

MARNIE: Because it's gonna be a gorgeous wedding. I'm gonna wear my Mom's wedding dress

it's from 1910 and her mom wore it

and her mom's mom wore it

and it's satin with inlaid pearls, well not inlaid pearls, that's not the word I'm, and I remember when I was a tiny girl I remember thinking "I gonna wear that dress" because it's the most, it's gorgeous and I'm gonna get to be looked at, I'm gonna,

Gary was just a prop. He was. He was just

And I knew he wanted me to say yes, so I did. I just

I kept lying

And then, worse, Frank, he suddenly he he changed on me.

FRANK: How?

MARNIE: He started acting like a husband. How he thinks a husband is, the world's dangerous and he has to protect me and that means I have to listen to him and he's gonna tell me what to do and I'm gonna have to act like he tells me. He's gonna be like his Dad. But his Mom's this little mousy woman who never says Boo. And I'm not gonna be her.

Uh uh.

But I just don't know what to say to Gary.

FRANK: Make something up.

MARNIE: I want to tell him the truth. I do.

FRANK: Well then tell it.

MARNIE: It's good you brought me here. I'm gonna need some help doing all this. Will you wait for me?

FRANK: Of course I will.

MARNIE: I'm gonna go sit and be quiet for a minute. You're so sweet. I
   wish I'd met you before I met Gary.
   (She goes offstage to the altar.)
   (Frank waits.)

EARTHQUAKE CHICA
Anne Garcia-Romero

Seriocomic
Esmeralda and Sam, twenties

> *Esmeralda and Sam work at a law firm. She is a secretary; he's an
> accountant. She doesn't care much for her Latino roots, whereas
> Sam does. She is fiery and outspoken; he is shy and timid. An
> unlikely couple to be sure!*

> *Lights rise on Esmeralda and Sam at an evening law firm
> Christmas party in a downtown high-rise.*

ESMERALDA: Earthquake. *(With Anglo accent.)* Terremoto. My father
called me that. I'm not an earthquake, alright? I'm a force of nature,
though. Watch me move.
(She does a sexy dance move.)
SAM: You're not an earthquake.
ESMERALDA: Then what am I?
SAM: A force of nature?
ESMERALDA: What kind?
(She does another sexy dance move. She blows him a kiss.)
SAM: Windstorm?
(She does another sexy dance move. She licks her lips.)
SAM: Rainfall?
(She does another sexy dance move. She sucks on her finger.)
SAM: A tidal wave?
(She stops dancing.)
ESMERALDA: I'm not a tidal wave.
SAM: Not a tidal wave . . . I mean you like to create waves . . . fantastic
waves . . . like the kind that surfers ride and revel in because they're
awesome surfers.
ESMERALDA: Drop it, Mister Accountant-Numbers Boy.

SAM: Sam.

ESMERALDA: I know your name. Don't worry, little Sammy, I catch the drift. So what's up with the slick hair, huh? Got a little spiffed up for ye old *(With over emphasized Anglo accent.) fiesta de navidad?*

SAM: You speak the language? Me too.

ESMERALDA: Nope. Before my dad died two months ago, his Latin face would erupt in anger, turn the color of bricks while he screamed at me. *(With Anglo accent.) "Terremoto. Terremoto."*

SAM: I'm sorry. My condolences.

ESMERALDA: You think I'd speak the language after that?

SAM: I . . . I don't know.

ESMERALDA: Yeah. Whatever. So what do ya' do to have fun, soldier? Are ya' kinky? Huh? Huh? Oh come on, I know your type. The silent numbers cruncher. You sit in this damn office all day long and you crunch, crunch, crunch, until your little fingers go numb and then you go home and put on your leather and hit the bars.

SAM: I uh . . . read . . . novels and poetry. Do math.

ESMERALDA: I said fun, soldier.

SAM: I uh . . . like devour Latin American literature and work on math equations in my spare time . . . algebra mostly.

ESMERALDA: But you do like leather, don't you?

SAM: Depends on what kind.

ESMERALDA: Now we're talkin'.

SAM: Leather bound editions of my favorite novels, sure. But the kind of leather you're talking about . . . I don't think so.

ESMERALDA: Come on, you'd look so hot in some chaps, a harness . . . with a fine black cap on your head. Oh yeah.
(She musses his hair.)

SAM: You have nice hands.

ESMERALDA: You have a nice ass.

SAM: I do? OK . . . um . . . but you . . . whenever you place your boss' time sheets in my in-box I notice how long and slender and delicate your fingers are.

ESMERALDA: Do you always wear your hair like that? It would look so much cuter if you did it like this. *(She plays with his hair.)* There. Much better. *(Beat.)* Do you get wasted on a regular basis because I don't. I can't. I joined one of those programs a few years ago but like I don't go anymore because I can't stand the people at those meetings and all their annoying lingo, but I know I can't drink. My body can't handle it.

SAM: I don't drink much. Only when I'm nervous.

ESMERALDA: What're you nervous about?

(Sam looks away nervously.)

ESMERALDA: Me? . . . The lowly worm secretary on the totem pole here?

SAM: But see you're fantastic because you don't care. You willingly buck the dress code and you talk loudly to the secretaries and the lawyers. You don't seem to care much about what people think at all.

ESMERALDA: OK, and you've had how much to drink?

SAM: Would you wanna . . . I mean . . . maybe we could, you know, have lunch together . . . sometime?

ESMERALDA: Oh please. You crunch numbers. I can barely type. It would never work.

SAM: Look, if you don't wanna get together during the week, maybe on a weekend day, we could you know, meet up for coffee or something.

ESMERALDA: You're too normal.

SAM: I could teach you some Spanish.

ESMERALDA: I tried. Didn't work. My father called me earthquake *chica.*

SAM: Alright then . . . uh . . .

ESMERALDA: "You are earthquake *chica*" He began to speak in Spanglish toward the end of his unhappy life.

SAM: Well . . . so . . . Merry Christmas. *Feliz Navidad y Prospero Año Nuevo. (He starts to walk away.)*

ESMERALDA: One time I saw this gypsy singer at this concert . . . she was like wailing in Spanish and I burst into tears, spontaneously. But I just kinda don't fit in. Got it?

(Sam stops.)

SAM: The language is inside of you, Esmeralda.

ESMERALDA: He even knows my name. You're a persistent little fella, aren't ya? This fiesta is so done. I'm outta here.

SAM: So are you gonna avoid me now that we've talked, like this?

ESMERALDA: Oh yeah, like I'm gonna run away screaming every time I see your face because you asked me out and I rejected you.

SAM: Whatever. I mean I've crossed that line from professional to personal.

ESMERALDA: Listen, pal, lines don't exist with me. I'm not a lines kinda gal. Got it? So I won't avoid you. I will talk to you. I just won't go out with you.

(Lights shift.)

EARTHQUAKE CHICA

Anne Garcia-Romero

Seriocomic
Esmeralda and Sam, twenties

> *Esmeralda and Sam work at a law firm. She is a secretary; he's an accountant. She doesn't care much for her Latino roots, whereas Sam does. She is fiery and outspoken; he is shy and timid. An unlikely couple to be sure!*

> *Lights rise on Esmeralda and Sam standing in a storage supply closet.*

ESMERALDA: I'm not hiding in here and having a lesson. If I were hiding in here it would be to do some fine UPS guy. Have you noticed how the delivery dudes always have completely chiseled calves and beautiful bulging biceps? But no, we're not here for that, are we?

SAM: Who says we're hiding?

ESMERALDA: We're standing in a storage supply closet with the door almost all the way closed.

SAM: We need supplies.

ESMERALDA: What . . . are we going on a field trip or something?

SAM: For our lessons. Now come on. Grab some. *(He grabs some supplies off the shelf.)*

ESMERALDA: I don't steal anymore. I gave that up with drinking and smoking.

SAM: Well, so I also brought you this.
    (Sam hands Esmeralda a book.)

ESMERALDA: *(With Anglo accent.)* Poesia y ficción.

SAM: *(With Spanish accent.)* Poesia y ficción.

ESMERALDA: Yeah. Right. Whatever.

SAM: An anthology of writers. Neruda. Lorca. Borges. Excerpts. Bilingual edition. *(Beat.)* And this . . .
    (Sam hands Esmeralda another book.)

ESMERALDA: Algebra for society. I think you're getting a little carried away here. I didn't say I wanted to become like a math whiz or anything.

SAM: It kind of reviews the basics. I wasn't sure where you stood with regard to exponents and binomials.

(Sam hands Esmeralda a clear plastic bag filled with sand.)

ESMERALDA: A bag of sand.

SAM: Serves several functions. The passing of time.

ESMERALDA: Did you take the bus down to the beach to get this sand? That is like so out of your way.

SAM: And the longer evolutionary view. Once boulders. Now sand.

ESMERALDA: Listen. Forget about it. I think you're way into this and making me into this project like I'm some kind of lame kid or something, like I can't think for myself. I graduated from high school. I got my certificate alright? I could've gone to college, but I didn't want to. I went to the college of life, alright? And just because you think you're gonna teach this poor little dumb ass girl who you're hot for so you'll condescend to her level, you're wrong. Where did you go to college anyway?

SAM: U.C.L.A.

ESMERALDA: Oh great. Just forget it.

SAM: What?

ESMERALDA: In a moment of weakness, I asked you for help. But I don't need your big ass university special ed help. And standing here in this storage closet with two large books and a bag of sand is certainly not what I had in mind.

(Sam start whistling.)

ESMERALDA: What? Now you're gonna teach me a little tune?

SAM: When I'm nervous, I whistle.

ESMERALDA: Again I make you nervous.

SAM: Yes, when you threaten to take back your request for lessons, something I've been looking forward to for the past twenty-three hours and seventeen minutes since you first mentioned it. This connection through language and numbers, native and acquired, intrigues me and gives me a sense of motivation and purpose and that's new for me. I'm nervous about losing that. Yes.

ESMERALDA: So you're not gonna be like mean? Because I can't stand that.

SAM: I never would be.

ESMERALDA: You know that movie with Audrey what's-her-name and that old English dude and he like transforms her? That's not what we're talking about here. Not at all. Got that?

SAM: Not at all. Can I read you a line or two?

ESMERALDA: Better be quick before one of the floor wardens breaks up our little love fest.

SAM: Neruda writes . . . *"Amo las cosa loca, locamente.* I have a crazy, crazy love of things. *Amos todas las cosas, no sólo las supremas, sino las infinitamente chicas.* I love all things, not only the grandest but also the infinitely tiny."

ESMERALDA: Alright.

SAM: Lorca writes . . . *"Mi corazón tendría la forma de un zapato sí cada aldea tuviera una sirena.* My heart would be shaped like a shoe if a mermaid would live in every village."

ESMERALDA: Uh-huh.

SAM: Neruda is crazy. Lorca's heart is moved by mermaids. You're in good company.

ESMERALDA: Whatever. I'm not crazy and I saw that movie about the mermaid played by that tall blonde chick and she likes falls in love with the guy. Puh-lease.

SAM: Borges writes . . . *"Sabia que su inmediata obligación era el sueño.* He knew his immediate duty was to dream."

ESMERALDA: I better get back to my desk before Mister Boss Man starts looking for me.

SAM: So, a binomial is an algebraic expression that is the sum or difference of two terms. An exponent is a symbol indicating what power of a factor is to be taken.

ESMERALDA: I didn't say I wanted any help in math, OK? I know how to use a calculator and that's about all the help I need.

SAM: But they say that if you're good in math, you can be good at learning a foreign language. I thought the Algebra could be a nice complement to the Spanish.

(The sounds of a copy machine echo into the storage room.)

ESMERALDA: The copy machine means one of the other mud slingers is close by which means this little lesson is over.

(Sam reaches into the plastic bag of sand.)

SAM: Have a pinch. To remind and guide you until the next lesson.

ESMERALDA: If it's my obligation to dream, maybe I dreamt this.

(Sam puts a pinch of sand in her palm.)

SAM: This sand reminds you that you are very much awake.

(Lights shift.)

(The following Saturday afternoon. Lights rise on Esmeralda and Sam standing inside a bare, studio apartment. Esmeralda paces.)

ESMERALDA: Solitary palm tree out the main window. One largish room. Smallish bathroom. Kitchenette. Decent closet. Fresh carpet and paint. Do I take it?

SAM: Do you want it?

ESMERALDA: I'm asking your opinion.

SAM: You want my opinion?

ESMERALDA: Ah . . . yes.

SAM: Well, for a studio apartment, this room does get strong sunlight.

ESMERALDA: But does it get good moonlight or starlight . . . so I can entertain in my mediumish bed?

SAM: You could grow things in here. Have an indoor garden.

ESMERALDA: I like plants. Ivy. Spider plant. Maybe some cacti too. *(Playfully seductive.)* Or should I pronounce it cock-tie?

SAM: *Tu jardin. La jardinera.* You could be an indoor gardener. I mean . . . just the other day I read an article in the paper about this kind of flower called Passiflora. It's purple with lace and white egg shaped fruit inside that's supposedly tasty.

ESMERALDA: What if I put my bed here? Would that be following that Chinese thing? Fung something? Or should I put it here? Does your head have to be facing the door? Is that so you can like lie naked in bed watching some totally hot dude enter your room and you're like, "Let's get it on, sucka"?

SAM: The passiflora were discovered by the conquistadores who thought the flower's parts reminded them of the passion of their Lord. It is a very metaphysical flower. Passion on many levels.

ESMERALDA: Are you saying I need more passion in my life?

SAM: You're doing just fine.

ESMERALDA: I know this no-sex platonic thing might be grating on your very last nerve but well, sorry, tough, you know?

SAM: *(Lying.)* It's not.

(The sound of a loud crash fills the room.)

ESMERALDA: God almighty. I can't handle this.

SAM: Just garbage trucks. Dumpsters.

ESMERALDA: God, am I gonna hear traffic noises all night going up and down the alley? Because you know I can't handle that. I am very sensitive to noises. And smells. If I smell garbage and like car fumes, I'll get very sick. And then I won't be able to work and I won't be able to afford the apartment.

SAM: It's a quiet alley. The noise and smells will pass.

ESMERALDA: Really?

SAM: I think so.

(An awkward beat.)

ESMERALDA: Right, I mean it's not that you're not attractive really. I mean, you know, in a normal sort of way . . .

SAM: I said we don't have to . . .

ESMERALDA: It's just I don't wanna get into it with you and we have like two weeks of doing it in all these amazing positions and then you get all needy and I'm like whatever and then there's this fight and you hate me and you bail and it sucks and we never talk again and then it's the same old shit.

SAM: The way your mind works. The way your hands move when your thoughts flow. The ways your eyes dance when you tell your stories. Passion is there. You say you can't speak the language when it's in the very fabric of your existence.

ESMERALDA: Alright. Thank you, oh wise one.

SAM: Passion takes on many forms. Flower. Mind. Hands. Eyes. Thoughts. And of course, the more conventional. But I'm not a very conventional guy.

(A radio blares salsa as a car drives by and idles.)

ESMERALDA: I wanna go dancing tonight.

SAM: As you know, I don't dance.

(An awkward beat.)

ESMERALDA: Come on. You have to at least know a few little moves or two, Sammy.

SAM: Not really.

ESMERALDA: Come on.

SAM: I'd rather not.

ESMERALDA: I may not speak the language with my lips but my hips, baby, my hips.

SAM: Sorry.

ESMERALDA: Please?

SAM: Don't make me.

(The salsa music fades as the car drives away.)

ESMERALDA: OK.

SAM: I mean what I say, Esmeralda.

ESMERALDA: Got it.

SAM: You're used to certain ways of connecting and I can tell these ways no longer work for you.

ESMERALDA: I can't even dance anymore?

SAM: You know what I mean.

ESMERALDA: What? Here's the thing. Even if we did get involved and you didn't get completely freaked out after two weeks of our all night fuck festivals and we actually hit it off . . . eventually you'd lose interest or I'd overwhelm you and then you'd bolt. And I'm very tired of that. So don't pretend like you don't care or think about it because I know you do but it's like you'd be outta here in a month and then . . .

SAM: Don't misrepresent me. It sounds like you're the one who's afraid of losing interest.

ESMERALDA: OK, so maybe you're not like that but I know you have this agenda . . . like you wanna help me for some reason and look, if you think I'm gonna become some astrophysicist or Spanish guru after a few little lessons with you, you're wrong. I mean please, you're a lowly accountant who lives with his parents. You want to make me into this cultural intellectual mathematical wonder but it's not like that alright? It's not. And it won't be.

SAM: I should leave now. *(Beat.)* I'm not trying to make you into anything, Esmeralda. *(Beat.)* Rent this place. The sunlight will help.

ELECTION DAY
Josh Tobiessen

Comic
Edmund and Brenda, twenties

> *It's the day of the local election and Brenda is out putting up
> posters. She believes in participatory democracy; whereas Edmund
> may not even vote, it being a waste of time and all.*

> *Pine Nut Café. Brenda enters with a handful of flyers and posters.
> Edmund is working. Sort of.*

EDMUND: Welcome to the Pine Nut Café.

BRENDA: I've been here before. Do you mind if I put up some posters?

EDMUND: You in a band?

BRENDA: It's for the election today.

EDMUND: Well, check that wall. I think some of those shows are over.
Check the dates.

BRENDA: Thanks. I have some flyers too if there's some place that you
put those.

EDMUND: I can just put them by the counter.

BRENDA: That would be great. It's just for today.

EDMUND: Are you going to get something to eat?

BRENDA: Ah, I probably should, shouldn't I?

EDMUND: I think so.

BRENDA: OK, let me just think . . . *(Checks her watch.)*. Yeah, I have time.
If you could just tell them in the kitchen that I'm in a bit of a hurry.
(Brenda sits down at one of the tables.)

EDMUND: Busy day huh?

BRENDA: Busy busy busy. Because of the election.

EDMUND: OK.

BRENDA: Don't forget to vote!

EDMUND: Sure, right. You working for one of the guys?

BRENDA: Sure am. Don't worry I'm working for the good guy.

EDMUND: Good to hear.

BRENDA: Just thought you should know so you don't spit in my food or anything.

EDMUND: OK.

BRENDA: Sorry, that was a stupid thing to say. I'm not trying to imply that you would ever actually spit in anyone's food.

EDMUND: No, I do sometimes.

BRENDA: Oh, well then I'm glad I told you.

EDMUND: So our special today is a mushroom and leek lasagna. Were you ready to order?

BRENDA: Yes. Sorry, did you say you had voted or were going to vote?

EDMUND: Not yet. I've been here all morning. I will.

BRENDA: Make sure you do. It's important.

EDMUND: Sure. I mean, voting's fine, I agree. But I usually like to get a little more involved.

BRENDA: Oh good, what do you —

(Edmund holds up his wrist, which is bandaged.)

BRENDA: Ouch, what happened?

EDMUND: You want to know what happened?

BRENDA: Can you tell me?

EDMUND: Don't see why not. It was on TV. It's from handcuffs. I was chained to a tree in the Tolowa Forest for 29 hours. That's why I wasn't at work Friday.

BRENDA: Yeah, I remember that. How did it go?

EDMUND: Well, some of the trees were marked and some weren't, and we didn't know which ones were getting the saw so . . . We guessed wrong. You ready to order?

BRENDA: Sorry, yes. I'll have the barbequed eggplant and lentils.

EDMUND: Alright.

BRENDA: I was actually at that protest also.

EDMUND: Yeah?

BRENDA: Just so you know I sympathize with what you're doing. I mean, I wasn't up a tree or anything. That looked kind of dangerous.

EDMUND: It was. I used to write a ton of letters to the papers trying to get my point across, but no one reads anymore. Americans—and by

Americans I mean everyone in the world who owns a TV—love a spectacle. That's why they used that shot on the news. You want an iced tea with that?

BRENDA: Oh, you remembered — You know what? Maybe a glass of wine. One glass isn't going to hurt, right? I'm just putting up posters. Do you have a pinot grigio?

EDMUND: We have a house red and a house white.

BRENDA: The white sounds nice.

EDMUND: *(Writing.)* White wine.

BRENDA: So had you ever done that before? Chaining yourself to trees?

EDMUND: Yeah, we do that kind of thing a lot.

BRENDA: *We*, as in a group?

EDMUND: Yeah.

(Edmund shows Brenda his T-shirt with the letters T.R.E.E. on it.)

BRENDA: Tree?

EDMUND: Total Reclamation of Endemic Ecology.

BRENDA: Wow.

EDMUND: I'm the leader. I started it.

BRENDA: Good for you. So are you not a part of . . .

EDMUND: We were, but my group is better. We made these bracelets too.

BRENDA: *(Reading bracelet.)* Cool. 'Running Bear'?

EDMUND: That's my Native American name.

BRENDA: Oh, are you Native Ameri —

EDMUND: No. Not by blood.

BRENDA: Yeah I think I've heard of you before.

EDMUND: Wouldn't be surprised. I'm fairly active in the community.

BRENDA: That's crazy. I've been coming here for months. I didn't know that you were . . . I thought you were just some coffee guy. You have this whole other thing going on. Anything coming up with your group?

EDMUND: Maybe.

BRENDA: Maybe? Well, what I mean is, I'm fairly politically minded myself, so —

EDMUND: *(Shows her his shirt.)* Check out our website.

BRENDA: Hang on. *(Brenda takes out her blackberry and types the address.)* Alright, I will.

EDMUND: So the eggplant with lentils and a white wine?
BRENDA: That's right.
EDMUND: And I won't spit in it.
BRENDA: Thanks.
   (Lights.)

END DAYS
Deborah Zoe Laufer

Comic
Rachel and Nelson, teens

> *Rachel is rebelling against her eccentric parents by pretending to be a goth chick. Nelson is a new classmate who likes to dress up as Elvis, which gets him beaten up a lot. Here he is joining her for lunch.*

> *Nelson heads toward Rachel, struggling to hold his tray while maneuvering around a sling and a guitar. There is now a large bandage across the bridge of his nose.*

NELSON: Rachel! Hi! Mind if I join you?

RACHEL: *(Refusing to look up.)* Yes.

NELSON: Oh.

> *(He looks around blankly.)*

RACHEL: There's an empty table over there.

NELSON: OK.

> *(But he just stands there, silent for a moment. Then:)*
> You were so amazing this morning. At the blackboard. Had you worked out that equation before? Because you wrote it out so fast. It's like you were channeling it or . . . something . . .
> *(Rachel finally looks up at him.)*

RACHEL: What happened to your nose?

NELSON: This? Oh, I was just horsing around with some of the guys.

RACHEL: If you'd stop dressing like that, they might stop beating you up.

NELSON: No, no. We were just roughhousing. It was all in fun.
  . . . Anyway, Nurse Liz is real nice. Stopped the bleeding in about two seconds. Patched me right up.

RACHEL: Whatever.

> *(She goes back to her book.)*

NELSON: I was saying to your dad, it's too bad you're not taking physics. With your calculus, you'd be a natural.

RACHEL: Yeah. Look, don't come by my house any more, OK? And don't tell anybody about . . . anything at my house. OK?

NELSON: You can count on me, Rachel. What happens between us, stays between us.

RACHEL: Great.

(She goes back to her book. Barely acknowledges him through the following.)

NELSON: *(Trying to consult some notes, while balancing his tray.)* I can't believe how alike our houses are.

RACHEL: Uh huh.

NELSON: Have you lived there long?

RACHEL: No.

NELSON: Where are you from?

RACHEL: New York.

NELSON: New York City? Wow. You're from New York City. How great is that?

RACHEL: Great.

NELSON: Why did you move?

RACHEL: My dad lost his job.

NELSON: Oh. How did he . . .

RACHEL: It blew up when a plane flew into it.

NELSON: A plane . . . Wow. Was he OK?

RACHEL: Oh yeah. He's great.

. . . *(To Nelson.)*

Sit. Would you just sit for Christ's sake.

NELSON: Gee. Thanks.

(He eagerly sits down and starts eating his macaroni and cheese.)

They've got very good macaroni and cheese here. Much better than my last school. Less gooey.

RACHEL: I'd really like to just read, OK?

NELSON: Yeah? Me too. I love to read. Did you ever read this?

(He holds up his book. "A Brief History of Time.")

RACHEL: What is it?

NELSON: It's only the greatest book ever written.

RACHEL: What *is* it?

NELSON: Stephen Hawking explains pretty much everything in the universe.

RACHEL: Does he explain why you're dressed like that?

NELSON: No, you know, like all the great scientific theories from Aristotle and Ptolemy pretty much up until now.

RACHEL: Oh.

NELSON: You would love it.

RACHEL: I don't think so.

NELSON: No, you would — I mean, it all comes down to math. Unification. To have a mathematical equation that integrates Einstein's General relativity with Quantum mechanics. An equation that encompasses everything.

RACHEL: And then what?

NELSON: And then we know how it all works.

RACHEL: And then what?

NELSON: And then we can figure out how it all started.

RACHEL: And then what?

NELSON: Ummm. And then we know.

(Rachel goes back to her book.)

He's so amazing. Stephen Hawking. He's got A.L.S. — they told him he'd die when he was like twenty, and he's lived more than forty years past that and he rides around in a motorized wheelchair and he talks through a computer. It's like the greatest brain on the planet riding around on this chair. You want to borrow it?

RACHEL: No thanks.

NELSON: It's OK. I've got my name in the cover.

RACHEL: No.

NELSON: It's really easy. I mean, it's written in a way that anyone can understand.

(Pause.)

Come on. Take it. And then you can tell me what you think.

(She takes the book.)

Great! Wow! This is so great!

RACHEL: I probably won't read it.

NELSON: But you might.

RACHEL: I might.

NELSON: And then we could talk about it. Oh my God. That would be just about the greatest thing ever.

(Rachel looks at him for a long moment.)

RACHEL: You should stop wearing that outfit.

NELSON: That's OK.

RACHEL: They won't stop beating on you till you stop.

NELSON: I'm used to it.

RACHEL: But why get used to it? Why not just be normal?

NELSON: Why do you wear that outfit?

RACHEL: So people will leave me alone.

NELSON: Oh.

RACHEL: Clearly it's not working.

NELSON: Some people think he's like a savior or something. Elvis. That he didn't really die, or that he'll rise again.

RACHEL: They're nuts.

NELSON: Maybe. My mom loved him. She got me an Elvis outfit for Halloween when I was five and I would never take it off.

RACHEL: That was probably cute. When you were five.

NELSON: Yeah. So, I just kept wearing it. Everywhere. Even to my Mom's funeral I wore it. My dad finally threw it away and I wouldn't get dressed. Went to kindergarten in my underwear.

RACHEL: You're kidding.

NELSON: Nope. So eventually he got me a new one. I find it really comforting. We've got the same birthday. Elvis and I. January 8th. And guess who else has it?

RACHEL: Who?

NELSON: Guess.

RACHEL: No.

NELSON: Come on. Somebody amazing.

RACHEL: Just tell me for Christ sakes.

NELSON: Stephen Hawking! The guy I was just telling you about! The book guy.

RACHEL: So?

NELSON: Isn't that cool?

RACHEL: Maybe you should dress like him.

NELSON: It's OK. They always beat me up the first month or so. But it gets old after a while. I expect it'll stop soon.

GOD'S EAR

Jenny Schwartz

Dramatic
Mel and Ted, thirties

> *Mel and Ted are a married couple who have recently had a child.*
> *Ted has been travelling on business and has just come home.*

TED: I brought you something.

MEL: You shouldn't have.

TED: I wanted to.

MEL: Why?

TED: No reason.

MEL: You know I hate surprises.

TED: Why?

MEL: No reason.

TED: Now, close your eyes.

MEL: For what?

TED: For fun.

Now, open your eyes.

MEL: For what?

TED: For fun.

(He gives her the gift.)

MEL: Oh Ted, they're . . .

TED: Slippers.

MEL: Do they keep on giving?

TED: *(Meaning: do you like them?)* What do you think?

MEL: I love them, I think.

But I don't like them, I don't think.

I like the idea of them, I think.

But I don't like the expression of the idea of them, I don't think.

TED: I saw them in the store window, and I thought of you.

I thought they looked like you.

Like the way you used to look.

Before you bit your tongue.

MEL: Lip.

TED: Before you burned your tongue.

I can't talk.

I'm in a room full of people.

It's hot.

We're sweating through our suits.

MEL: And the women?

TED: There are no women.

MEL: And the hotel?

TED: It's alright.

MEL: How's your room?

TED: I suppose.

MEL: Wait.

TED: What?

MEL: Shh . . .

I'm trying to imagine the rest of my life without you . . .

Ted?

TED: Yes?

MEL: What's that around your ankle?

Is that a thong?

Is that a thong around your ankle?

Why is there a thong around your ankle?

Who does it belong to?

No don't tell me please don't tell me no don't tell me I don't want to know.

TED: Amanda.

It belongs to Amanda.

MEL: Does Amanda have a name?

TED: Tina.

MEL: Does Bridget have a name?

TED: Marie.

MEL: Does Chloe have a name?

TED: Sonya.

MEL: Does Hilary have a name?

TED: Gail.

MEL: Does Ellen have a name?

TED: Nancy.

MEL: Does Barbara have a name?

TED: Lourdes.

MEL: Does Ingrid have a name?

TED: Lenora.

MEL: I only know one Lenora.

The electrician, this morning, he gave the dog the finger.

There's a child in this house, I said.

We don't use that finger.

TED: How is the dog?

MEL: Ask her yourself.

TED: How is the dog?

MEL: She doesn't exist as far as the cat's concerned.

TED: How is the dog?

MEL: Needy.

She thinks I'm going to leave her.

I can't imagine why.

TED: How is the dog?

MEL: Clever.

She thinks you get Lyme Disease from limes.

TED: How is the dog?

MEL: Bloated.

She thinks food is love and love is food and love is food and food
is love.

TED: How is the dog?

MEL: She has a feeling we're not in Kansas anymore.

TED: How is the dog?

MEL: Pissy.

She's given up caffeine.

She's gone cold turkey.

TED: And you?

MEL: I turned on the TV and lit a cigarette.

TED: Just one?

MEL: Yes.

TED: Two?

MEL: Yes.

TED: Six?

MEL: Yes.

TED: Ten?

MEL: Did you go to duty free?

Did you buy cigarettes?

TED: I did.

I tried.

There was a line.

MEL: Did you forget?

TED: I never forget.

MEL: You were early.

You could have waited.

TED: I was starving —

MEL: *Go ahead!*

Starve!

See if I care!

See if I notice that you're gone!

See if I wonder if you're ever coming back!

Are you ever coming back?

See if I care!

See if I care!

See if I notice that you're gone!

There's an echo.

Do you hear it?

There's an echo.

Do you hear it?

See if I care!

See if I notice that you're gone!

(He kisses her tenderly. Holds her. She lets him. Lets her go.)

TED: I kissed you this morning, but you didn't wake up.

Like that.

But with more tenderness.

If you can imagine more tenderness.

MEL: Was I dreaming?

TED: I don't know.

MEL: I must have been dreaming.

TED: I don't know.

MEL: Did you ever have that dream?
     Where you're falling?
     And your organs are suspended?
     And there's nowhere to go, but down?

TED: You're cold.

MEL: Let's go inside.
     I'm cold.

TED: We are inside.

MEL: What about the dog?

TED: What about the cat?

MEL: Danger: Chlamydia.
     Again.

TED: Not again.

MEL: What about the bunny?

TED: We don't have a bunny.

MEL: Did you ever have that dream?

TED: I'm having it now.
     Oh well.

MEL: Oh well what?

TED: I'll call you when I land.

MEL: The man in the shop, he sold me a killer fish.
     I still haven't cleaned out the tank.
     I can't.
     I won't do it.
     If it's the last thing I don't do.

TED: I brought you something.

MEL: You shouldn't have.

TED: I wanted to.

MEL: Why?

TED: No reason.

MEL: You know I hate surprises.

TED: Why?

MEL: No reason.

TED: Now, close your eyes.

MEL: For what?

TED: For fun.

Now, open your eyes.

MEL: For what?

TED: For fun.

(He gives her the gift.)

MEL: Oh Ted, they're . . .

TED: Milk Duds.

MEL: Do they keep on giving?

TED: In case you forgot the day I fell in love with you.

MEL: You know I have a weakness for anything sweet . . .

Lenora from high school.

She was the star of all the plays.

Is your Lenora the star of all the plays?

THE LAST BARBECUE
Brett Neveu

Dramatic
Barry and Kathy, late twenties

> *Barry is married. Kathy is his ex-girlfriend who has showed up for a barbecue in Barry's parents' back yard. They haven't seen each other in ten years, not since high school.*

> *Lights up. The chairs and the grill are out. The cooler is still out, and so is the Frisbee. A few beats. Barry and Kathy enter.*

BARRY: The cooler's still out.

KATHY: Were your folks having a party?

BARRY: I can't believe they just left this thing sitting here.

KATHY: Is there beer in there?

BARRY: You want a beer?

KATHY: Sure.

BARRY: OK. *(He opens the cooler. He pulls out two beers. They are dripping wet.)* It's a little warm.

KATHY: Thanks.

BARRY: I hope it's OK.

KATHY: It's fine.

BARRY: Hell, we've been drinking warm beer all night.

KATHY: That's true.

BARRY: I mean at the reunion they had warm beer.

KATHY: Yeah.

BARRY: I can't believe that I drank all of that warm beer!

KATHY: Yeah.

BARRY: But it was free, so what can you do. *(Pause.)* It's a nice night.

KATHY: Yeah.

BARRY: Are you getting bit up?

KATHY: No.

BARRY: I could light a citronella candle.

KATHY: I'm fine.

BARRY: Here. *(He exits towards house.)*

(A few beats.)

(Barry enters with a citronella candle. He lights it.)

BARRY: Here. *(He puts the candle on the ground.)*

That should keep them away.

KATHY: Thanks.

BARRY: My mom got them for the barbecue. They had a barbecue.

KATHY: Oh.

BARRY: You got into town last night?

KATHY: Yeah.

BARRY: And you're over at the Heartland?

KATHY: Yeah.

BARRY: That place is brand new.

KATHY: Today I just drove around looking at the town.

BARRY: Is it weird coming from New York and then back here?

KATHY: It's strange.

BARRY: I think it would be strange.

KATHY: I really didn't know what to think.

BARRY: I think it has to be strange.

KATHY: I saw my therapist five times this past week.

BARRY: Oh.

KATHY: I didn't know what to think about this whole thing, so I got worked up about being back, and so I kept calling my therapist and making appointments and trying to figure out why I was getting so nervous. I just kept thinking about it.

BARRY: It must be weird seeing everyone.

KATHY: I don't know.

BARRY: Are you hungry?

KATHY: Not really.

BARRY: Did you see the cheese and who knows what else over on that little table? I ate maybe one of those things. They were getting all sweaty just sitting out there by the bar. I thought maybe I was going to get sick! *(Pause.)* Man, did you see Jason Yardly?

KATHY: Who?

BARRY: Jason Yardly. He looked different.

KATHY: Jason Yardly?

BARRY: Someone told me he was the hit of the reunion.

KATHY: What does that mean?

BARRY: He had changed so much that it was so weird.

KATHY: Oh.

BARRY: It's weird that I still live here and you live in New York.

KATHY: I just ended up there.

BARRY: I know. I should come out there sometime. I think that it would be different. I would like to see what it's like out there.

KATHY: It's OK.

BARRY: Do you like your job?

KATHY: Yeah.

BARRY: It would be so great to do what you do.

KATHY: I like it.

BARRY: A pharmaceutical rep.

KATHY: I'm busy.

BARRY: And you get to travel.

KATHY: Yeah.

BARRY: That's interesting.

KATHY: It's just something different.

BARRY: Did you see that guy dancing on the table?

KATHY: No.

BARRY: Tim Mortenson was dancing on the table.

KATHY: Oh.

BARRY: He was drunker than shit!

KATHY: I missed it.

BARRY: He nearly fell on his ass.

KATHY: I didn't see it.

BARRY: It was pretty ironic with you and Tammy and Mark and David and me all standing there talking! I didn't think that would ever happen.

KATHY: Why?

BARRY: Everything that has happened between all of us, and how things are now. It was strange that there we were all talking to each other.

KATHY: That was a long time ago.

BARRY: But it was weird how we were all talking like nothing ever happened.

KATHY: We're older now.

BARRY: But it was so intense. I mean all of those relationships and all of those different feelings. All of those good times.

KATHY: Oh.

BARRY: It was great to see most of those people. Some of them were still assholes. It's interesting how much most people haven't changed.

KATHY: It's only been ten years.

BARRY: You just said that it was a long time ago.

KATHY: That's true.

BARRY: It's interesting, isn't it?

KATHY: Everyone pretty much looked the same.

BARRY: I meant more than looks. Everyone treated each other the same.

KATHY: I don't know.

BARRY: They did.

KATHY: I feel I've changed.

BARRY: You look the same.

KATHY: I've changed some in ten years. Basically, I'm the same. But I've changed some.

BARRY: Jason Yardly changed. People thought he looked great.

KATHY: Did you talk to him?

BARRY: I'm glad *we're* talking.

KATHY: Did you think we wouldn't talk to each other?

BARRY: I wasn't sure.

KATHY: I had more of a problem just coming to town than seeing any one individual.

BARRY: Oh.

KATHY: And you're married.

BARRY: I've really calmed down since high school.

KATHY: Oh.

BARRY: I'm not such an asshole.

KATHY: You shouldn't be so hard on yourself.

BARRY: Oh.

KATHY: It's hard being here.

BARRY: Yeah.

KATHY: Being here made me feel so uptight. I would get so rigid.

BARRY: Everyone there seemed to be doing real well.

KATHY: I don't know. Some of them looked old.

BARRY: I guess.

KATHY: Some of them looked like shit.

BARRY: I guess so.

KATHY: I got cornered by Kim Norvell over by the bar and she started to ask me all kinds of questions. She first started saying how she lived in New York and how she didn't like it. She said she had lived right outside of the city and how it was just not something she could get used to, then she started talking about Omaha or something and then she practically started apologizing for living here now, because she lives here now with her husband and two kids, and then complaining at the same time about New York! She was wondering how I live there and saying that she would have lived there if she could have handled it but she is so glad to live here now. She didn't know why she would have thought she could have lived anywhere else. She loves it here. She completely freaked me out. I didn't know how to respond.

BARRY: Wow.

KATHY: I just didn't know what to say.

BARRY: That's weird.

KATHY: I really was speechless.

BARRY: Weird.

KATHY: Then she just walked away. She had this lost look in her eyes and she walked away.

BARRY: Kim Norvell.

KATHY: It might have been someone else.

BARRY: Oh.

KATHY: I don't know.

BARRY: Huh.

KATHY: I just feel weird about the whole thing.

BARRY: It was fun, though, wasn't it?

KATHY: I don't know.

BARRY: Where did you drive around today?

KATHY: Around the town.

BARRY: Did you go to Martin Park?

KATHY: No.

BARRY: They have a new waterslide complex over there. They tore out the old slide and put in a new one towards the back, then they put in new showers and then out in the pool they put in these table / sprinkler things that you can sit down at and get wet at the same time. So I guess if you're hot then you can sit there and cool off and you don't have to swim if you don't want to. It really looks nice. It looks much better than it used to.

KATHY: Great.

BARRY: They had some zoning problems and they had some problems with some of the old people who didn't want to change anything. They wanted it to be the same as when it was built. It looks so much better, I don't know what they were thinking.

KATHY: They probably went swimming there when they were younger.

BARRY: It used to smell like piss.

KATHY: Oh.

BARRY: In the shower stalls, people must have pissed in there for fifty years because the bricks smelled like piss. It was sick.

KATHY: I don't remember.

BARRY: We went there a few times.

KATHY: We did?

BARRY: We went swimming.

KATHY: Good.

BARRY: Good?

KATHY: I'm sure I'd remember going if I thought about it.

BARRY: John Pretzer was a lifeguard.

KATHY: I'm sure I'd remember.

BARRY: What kind of things do you do in New York?

KATHY: I don't know.

BARRY: There's enough to do.

KATHY: That's true.

BARRY: Do you go out to eat?

KATHY: Sometimes.

(Pause.)

BARRY: Is your beer too warm?

KATHY: It's OK.

BARRY: I could get you a cold one out of the fridge if you want.

KATHY: No.

BARRY: OK.

    (Pause.)

KATHY: I noticed that the Big Bear closed.

BARRY: That closed five years ago.

KATHY: I used to get boots there.

BARRY: You did?

KATHY: These big rubber boots with buckles that would get frozen. They had a weird gray felt lining and would take hours to dry.

BARRY: That's so funny!

KATHY: I know! Isn't that funny?

BARRY: Yeah!

KATHY: My toes would get cold.

BARRY: I hate that.

KATHY: It was awful. I hated it.

BARRY: I hate that, too.

KATHY: It's too bad that the Big Bear closed.

BARRY: Yeah. Nollens closed. A few other places closed.

KATHY: Oh.

BARRY: Yeah.

KATHY: I think I'd like a cold beer now.

BARRY: Do you want a cold beer?

KATHY: Yes please.

BARRY: OK. I'll be right back.

    (Barry exits quickly towards the house.)

LINNEA
John Regis

Dramatic
Danny and Linnea, twenties

> *Danny is an aspiring young writer. He has become infatuated with an "exotic dancer" named Linnea who appears to like him, too. Of course, he is being set up for a fall.*

> *Linnea has entered, and now stands surveying the scene. She is in her early twenties, but seems older — a tall, linear girl, with cat-green eyes and a sallow tomboyish face and smile. Her nearly platinum blonde hair is streaked with dark roots. She wears a red minidress and heels. Danny stares blankly at her.*

LINNEA: Don't mind them. They're a couple of clowns.

DANNY: I — I don't.

LINNEA: I saw you watching me as I danced.

DANNY: Yes. I, eh . . . I'm sorry.

LINNEA: Don't apologize. We do it to be watched.

DANNY: Yea . . . it's just . . . I couldn't not watch.

LINNEA: I know.

DANNY: I — I felt drawn to you. Like you were beckoning me.

LINNEA: *(Laughing.)* Maybe I did beckon you. *(A slight pause.)* What's your name, honey?

DANNY: Danny.

LINNEA: Danny, will you buy me a drink? That way we can sit and talk?

DANNY: Sure.

> *(Linnea offers him her arm. Danny escorts her past the now-quieted Clown table. Susan, in the know, exits back through the curtains. The two sit. Linnea lights a cigarette. She will chain-smoke one cigarette after another in the scene. After a moment of silence.)*

LINNEA: So Danny —

DANNY: Yes?

LINNEA: Why did you cry out when I appeared?

DANNY: I was surprised to see you.

LINNEA: But you knew my name. How is that?

DANNY: Cody Marlin told me about you.

LINNEA: Cody Marlin! Are you a friend of Cody's?

DANNY: Not really. I just met him this evening. He showed me the sketch he'd done of you. I was very struck by it.

LINNEA: Were you? So you decided to come have a look for yourself?

DANNY: *(Embarrassed.)* Well, I . . .

LINNEA: And now that you've seen me, what do you think?

DANNY: *(Quietly.)* No drawing could have prepared me for this.

LINNEA: Why, that's very sweet of you, Danny. You know, I feel like I've seen you somewhere before. Is this your first time here?

DANNY: Yes.

LINNEA: So, drawings aside, we've never actually met?

DANNY: *(Laughing.)* I didn't say that!

LINNEA: What, we have met? Where? Perhaps the East Village?

DANNY: *(Almost inaudible.)* Perhaps in a dream.

LINNEA: A dream? *(Laughing.)* Why, Danny, you're a madcap!

DANNY: A what?

LINNEA: A madcap little dreamer with pixie dust in his eyes!

DANNY: *(Laughing.)* It's true. I know so little of real life; I can't help living my life as if it were a dream. Tonight, in particular, I've felt that way. But, even in my wildest dreams, I never thought I'd be here, talking with you.

LINNEA: There's a reason for that, Danny.

DANNY: Oh?

LINNEA: *(Leans in closer to him.)* Yes. You see . . . I'm a madcap too.
(The two stare at each other. Susan returns with Linnea's drink. Danny pays for it.)

LINNEA: I just had an idea, Danny.

DANNY: What?

LINNEA: Well, it's very slow tonight. Hardly worth the effort. I mean, I'd really rather sit and talk with you. Get the chance to know you. Of course, once I finish this drink, I have to go back on the floor.

DANNY: Oh . . . I see.

LINNEA: So, what I'm thinking of doing is blowing off the rest of work. I'll tell them — I don't know — I'll tell them I'm not feeling well. That way I'll be free the rest of the night. Get my drift, Danny?

DANNY: Not really.

LINNEA: Then I'll spell it out for you. I like you, Danny, and I think you're cute. I think it was fated we meet. I mean, we're madcaps, aren't we?

DANNY: Y-yes.

LINNEA: Now, don't get the wrong idea. I've never done this before. I mean, I wouldn't dream of doing this with any of the other clowns here. But you're different, Danny, I sense that.

DANNY: Doing what, Linnea?

LINNEA: Look, I'll just come out and say it. Would you like to go out with me? Maybe go back to the East Village and hit some bars, play some pool? It will be fun. What do you say, Danny? Two madcaps out on a tear?

(Pause.)

DANNY: All right.

LINNEA: You will?

DANNY: Yes.

LINNEA: You're sure?

DANNY: I'd love to.

LINNEA: Great!

(A pause.)

LINNEA: Now, look Danny, I'm going to ask you to front me some money. Say, eighty dollars? Now, it's not what you think! It's just, you know, I'm not working the rest of my shift, and I'm a little short. Look upon it as a loan. I mean, the next time will be my treat.

(A pause.)

DANNY: I, eh . . . I'll have to find a bank machine.

LINNEA: There's one near by. Here's what we gotta do. We can't just walk out together. That's frowned upon.

DANNY: I . . . I understand.

LINNEA: I'm going to get up now. I'll go tell them I'm leaving. They may ask me to dance one final dance. Meantime, finish up your beer.

Walk out of here, cross back over the highway, and then go up two blocks on Twelfth Avenue. There's a Chinese takeout on the northeast corner. Wait for me there. I'll come by in a cab in ten minutes. OK?

DANNY: I just have to make sure and find a bank machine.

LINNEA: We'll find a bank machine. *(A slight pause.)* You promise to wait for me?

DANNY: I promise.

LINNEA: Good man! See you in ten minutes. *(Exits.)*

MARIE ANTOINETTE: THE COLOR OF FLESH

Joel Gross

Dramatic
Elisa and Alexis, twenties

> *Elisa is official portrait painter to the Queen of France. Alexis is an impoverished aristocrat who is in love with her. Here, she urges him to become the Queen's lover, which she thinks will further his political career.*

> *That night, July 1777. Elisa's bedroom at her townhouse in Paris. Alexis sits on the edge of the bed, lost in thought. Elisa sits up and stretches with happy sensuality.*

ELISA: One thing I'll say about this American Revolution. It makes for magnificent farewells. *(Alexis finds his pants and begins to struggle into them. Elisa, who does not want him to go, covers her chagrin.)* Now it's your turn, Alexis. You say, "Yes, darling. And I've never in my life felt such passion —"

ALEXIS: "Yes, darling." *(Turning to her fully.)* You really are the most beautiful woman in Paris.

ELISA: In that case, you must be the least romantic man in Paris, leaving me in the middle of the night. *(Seeing that he is looking for his shoes.)* The servants will give me hell in the morning if you wake them on the way out.

ALEXIS: I've given those shiftless slugs fatter bribes than they deserve.

ELISA: Spoken like a true friend of the masses. *(Throws her arms around his neck from behind.)* Now come back and be nice to a member of the *nouveau riche.*

ALEXIS: I'm going to miss you, Elisa.

ELISA: Spend the night. *(Alexis finds his shoes.)* If you're thinking about my so-called husband, he's not due back for at least a week. You could stay here until it's time to ship out.

ALEXIS: *(Putting on his shoes.)* I was not thinking about your husband.

ELISA: What were you thinking about? *(She pulls him towards her lovingly.)* When you nearly put me on fire a moment ago?

ALEXIS: "Nearly"?

ELISA: I beg your pardon. I burned. It was a conflagration.

ALEXIS: I was thinking about the Queen.

ELISA: *(Offended.)* Thank you.

ALEXIS: Not at the actual moment when we —

ELISA: Very flattering, Alexis. Close your eyes and pretend you're deflowering our national virgin.

ALEXIS: Darling, I am sailing for America in two days.

ELISA: It's only an hour by fast coach to Versailles. Plenty of time. Think of it as your patriotic duty. The King cannot rise to the occasion. Only you can give the nation what it truly deserves: a bastard princeling, son of our over-indulged big-jawed Queen.

ALEXIS: If this is the way you, her friend, speak of her, what do you expect the common people — ?

ELISA: I expect common people make love to each other without any visions of Toinette getting in the way.

ALEXIS: It's a wonder the people have any strength to make love at all.

ELISA: Let's not start in with the people.

ALEXIS: Tonight, I found a mother nursing her infant in a stable.

ELISA: Too bad you're not a painter. You missed a superb opportunity for a "Holy Mother and Child."

ALEXIS: I don't look at these people as subjects for your canvases. I look at —

ELISA: Perhaps you should get to know some of them, Alexis. So that they might be more real to you than pathetic pictures in your mind, controversial talk for your dinner table. You might learn how this saintly mother got her baby in the first place, how she ended up in that stable.

ALEXIS: In your stable, Elisa.

ELISA: In my — ! Why do you tell me this now? Did you drive her away? *(Off his outraged look.)* She has no right — !

ALEXIS: There's plenty of room, if you schedule it properly. When you're being driven to the opera, mother and child can nap in the horse dung.

ELISA: For the love of God, Alexis, don't do this to me.

ALEXIS: When you return to your elegant new house just before dawn, glutted with champagne, sated with pleasure, they'll gladly come crawling out to make room for your noble horses. If you feel guilty, throw them some kitchen scraps.

ELISA: I don't feel guilty! Why the hell should I feel — ? *(Getting control of herself.)* Two topics I would like you to leave behind the next time you deign to visit my bed: the common people and the Queen of France. *(Throws him his cravat.)* Why don't you just go? You've eaten your dinner, you've enjoyed your sex — you've even managed to finish spouting another little oration about the poor. Go! Go to America with the other rich boys! Play soldier! Enjoy yourself! It's what you do best, isn't it?

ALEXIS: There will be change, Elisa. Change is unavoidable.

ELISA: Wonderful! I'm the first member of my family to have a servant — just in time for the revolution! What right do you have to preach about the destitute? You've never worked a day in your life.

ALEXIS: It is my class that must give voice to those unable to speak.

ELISA: It is your class that the mob will be the first to destroy. As far as I'm concerned, the American Revolution is practice for one of our own.

ALEXIS: Not if there's reform.

ELISA: You can't reason with peasants rioting for bread!

ALEXIS: First feed them.

ELISA: You're a hopeless dreamer! Workers are setting their own factories on fire. Garbage pickers throw rocks at noble carriages. Paupers are sleeping in my stable! *(Explaining.)* I grew up eating soup and apples for dinner, six times a week. You know what kept me from throwing rocks at rich carriages? Fear. You know what led me to riches? Desire. If you give the rabble what they lack, they'll only want more.

ALEXIS: You are wrong.

ELISA: You see what you want to see. You don't know them, because you've never been one of them.

ALEXIS: When people are free, they will behave with respect for their fellow man.

ELISA: Wait till you see how they behave in America. You'll probably be stabbed for your silver shoe buckles.

ALEXIS: Thank you for your concern. I shall watch my back.

ELISA: I hate you! . . . I hate you! *(Elisa strikes at him with her fists, but he grabs her flailing arms easily. Alexis kisses her, and though she resists wildly at first, the kiss slowly dissolves her anger. Gradually, she stops fighting him, returning his kiss with passion.)* You know if you went to your cousin in Normandy for a few months, rumors about you and the Queen would stop.

ALEXIS: That is not the reason I go to America.

ELISA: Why then? Have you used up all the women in France? *(Warning him.)* Colonials are notoriously ugly, Alexis.

ALEXIS: Good, it will keep my mind on the war.

ELISA: The Queen begged me to get you to stay in France. I can't even get you to stay overnight . . . You swear you'll come back to me, Alexis?

ALEXIS: Yes.

ELISA: All your limbs intact? Swear it!

ALEXIS: All my limbs.

ELISA: *(Admonishing him.)* No scars! *(Smoothing her hand across his face.)* Like peaches and cream.

ALEXIS: I will be home in a few months, Venus, weighted down with medals from the democratic American nation. *(He kisses her hand tenderly. Then, closely watched by Elisa, he finishes dressing in his elaborate uniform, and stands at the side of the bed.)* I made a grave error when I first fell in love with you, and asked you to run away with me. I never entertained the possibility of marriage.

ELISA: *(Deflecting his sentimentality.)* What am I going to do without you, Alexis?

ALEXIS: Not because you were married, but because of your class. I never imagined you as a potential wife, a countess. Forgive me for my idiotic prejudice, my blindness. *(Seriously.)* I want you to know that if you were not married, I would instantly offer you my hand.

ELISA: And I want you to know, that if I were George Washington, I would instantly make you a general. *(They share a laugh. Suddenly he takes her hands, needing her alliance desperately. He makes his request.)*

ALEXIS: Darling, speak to the Queen. *(Marie Antoinette, her hair disordered, dressed in undergarments, enters and stares downstage.)*

ELISA: I don't believe her story, Alexis.

ALEXIS: When she came to France, they stripped away every article of clothing she wore, even her undergarments. Everything had to be French. All her Austrian servants were sent home. She had to rip out every vestige of her childhood, of her happy life. She never met Louis until the day she married him. In a cathedral filled with a thousand strangers, chattering in a language she was still struggling to learn. Toinette was fifteen. Help her.

ELISA: No one remains a virgin after seven years of marriage.

ALEXIS: Our fates all hang together, my dear. The people will rejoice when the King has a son. A happy people do not rebel against just authority. Teach her. She doesn't understand — anything. *(Pause.)* You will be her lifelong friend.

ELISA: Do you think my friendship with the Queen is still based on selfishness and greed?

ALEXIS: I don't think so, Elisa. But I'm afraid that you do. No matter what you may say, I know that you love her.

ELISA: Have you actually made me a proposal of marriage, Alexis?

ALEXIS: Yes. *(Pause.)* After a fashion. *(Pause.)* What I mean is that because your husband is still alive, and I am going into a war on the other side of the world —

ELISA: It would be premature to have my bed-linens embroidered with your coat of arms.

ALEXIS: Elisa, you would make a wonderful countess.

ELISA: Yes. *(Pause.)* I'll talk to the Queen.

ALEXIS: Thank you, darling. *(Alexis starts to exit.)*

ELISA: Be careful. You're too beautiful to be a soldier. *(As he exits, Elisa calls after him from the bed.)* I love you, Alexis.

NONE OF THE ABOVE
Jenny Lyn Bader

Seriocomic
Clark, twenties; Jamie, teens

> *Clark has been hired by Jamie's parents to tutor her for her SATs,*
> *which she doesn't seem to care much about. She's more interested in*
> *his personal history.*

> *Clark is scanning the vocabulary book, testing Jamie.*

CLARK: Alright, how about . . . Mendacious. Define mendacious.

JAMIE: Damn I knew this yesterday. Don't you dare say I told you so!

CLARK: Did I . . . say anything? I asked you a word. You just don't
remember it because you're not wired on caffeine today.

JAMIE: *(Curious.)* What do you get wired on?

CLARK: Girls who do their homework.

JAMIE: *(Remembering her homework.)* Oh, uh —
(She hands it to him.)

CLARK: *(Checking it quickly.)* How did you get twelve here? And don't tell
me that the answer is always twelve.

JAMIE: I multiplied? You know, you never told me how you met
Margaret. I tell you everything, and then you completely withhold
from me.
(Clark stands, determined.)

CLARK: Jamie. You are never going to get a problem like this one wrong
again.

JAMIE: That's impossible.

CLARK: I know it seems impossible to you right now. But it's like . . .
Climbing a mountain. What appears to be completely impossible at
first, the rock face that looks vertical from below, the steepest part of
the incline — that face always looks different when you're at the

top, looking down, doesn't it? And you can only see, after you've done it, how you did it.

(*Jamie looks at him blankly.*)

You have climbed a mountain, haven't you?

JAMIE: I'm from New York. Where would we find a mountain?

CLARK: Upstate, maybe?

JAMIE: Is that where you're from?

CLARK: Yes. That's where I'm from.

JAMIE: So you were raised, like outdoors? Scaling mountains?

(*Clark stares at her.*)

I'm just asking, because, it's interesting. Exotic. I mean, there's nothing to scale here.

CLARK: Sure there is. You just have to be more inventive.

JAMIE: You mean like the rock wall at the Reebok club?

CLARK: Like that. OK. Take this problem. What are the main numbers here?

JAMIE: Where are you from exactly in the mountains? A farm?

CLARK: I'm from a small town. You've never heard of it.

JAMIE: How small?

CLARK: So small, there were no nightclubs!

JAMIE: Wow, so where did people hang out?

CLARK: The bar.

JAMIE: *The* bar? There was only one bar in your town?

CLARK: Yup. That's how small it was.

JAMIE: But what if you got carded? Where could you hang out?

CLARK: No one got carded. Everyone just drank from a young age. Are you looking at the problem?

JAMIE: You must be glad you moved here.

CLARK: That's debatable. What are the main numbers here?

JAMIE: A small town, huh? Did you call yourselves townies?

CLARK: Townies don't call themselves townies.

JAMIE: So what drove everyone to drink from a young age?

CLARK: I don't know. Maybe the despair of having only one bar?

JAMIE: You must have had an interesting childhood.

CLARK: Not as interesting as yours.

JAMIE: How old were you when you realized that you count words and numbers compulsively?

CLARK: Seven.

JAMIE: Were you on a mountain?

CLARK: *(Remembering.)* I was under a table. Hiding. Listening to my parents argue. I thought if I could count the number of words, they couldn't be infinite. They would have to end.

JAMIE: Did it work?

(A beat as he doesn't answer, and she understands it didn't work.)

CLARK: What are the main numbers here?

JAMIE: Clark? Do you just think about the SAT all the time so you won't have to deal with your real problems?

CLARK: What are the main numbers?

(Jamie stares at Clark, mesmerized. He is completely focused in a way she has never seen before.)

JAMIE: Um, there's three kumquats . . . and four pineapple wedges. So: three and four.

CLARK: What's three plus four?

JAMIE: Seven.

CLARK: What's three times four?

JAMIE: Twelve.

CLARK: Good! Now we eliminate the seven and twelve as answers! See, a lot of students just add or multiply. But the obvious answer is never right.

JAMIE: Are you serious? They put the seven and twelve there to trick people?

(Clark nods. Jamie looks at the test.)

Oh my god! These are all phony answers!

CLARK: They're not phony Jamie, they're —

JAMIE: They're attempts by the people in New Jersey to fuck with us!

CLARK: People in New Jersey?

JAMIE: Do you realize Educational Testing Services is in New Jersey? That's why they do this. They resent being in New Jersey.

CLARK: Jamie, they're in Princeton. Why would they resent being in Princeton? It's quite beautiful.

JAMIE: Not if your father wants you to go to school there. Then it's just like the rest of New Jersey, except with eating clubs.

CLARK: Look these over. I want you to cross out the two obvious wrong answers. Quickly. Go!

(She starts crossing out answers.)

Don't hesitate. Follow your gut. Look for the trick. Yes. Good. Keep going.

JAMIE: How'm I doing?

CLARK: Do you know, you've never asked me that?

JAMIE: I never knew the test people were trying to trick me! This is outrageous! I'm gonna show them!

CLARK: Circle the ones you think are right.

(She keeps going. Clark paces, coaching:)

The obvious answer is never right. The right answer is never obvious. Would you rather be impulsive or right?

JAMIE: I don't know! I love being impulsive! But I want to be right.

CLARK: Great. Now let's try it with Reading.

JAMIE: *(Horrified.)* There are fake answers in Reading too?

CLARK: There are fake answers everywhere.

(Jamie looks miserable as she stares at the page.)

What's wrong?

JAMIE: *(Tearful:)* Some of these passages, I don't know half the vocab. These words make me want to crawl into bed. Quit school. Quit everything.

CLARK: I can get you through it.

(Jamie shakes her head.)

JAMIE: "Penelope is a pedestrian, perambulating across a street. She sees a horse dashing past her at a manic pace."

(Jamie looks up:)

Just a typical day at the S.A.T.

(Returns to reading the passage:)

"Penelope makes a sarcastic comment."

(Looks up again.)

I don't blame her. Let's see . . . "A" looks right.

CLARK: That's why it's wrong!

JAMIE: Oh no!

CLARK: Just because she's "a" pedestrian doesn't mean she "is" pedestrian, see?

JAMIE: *(Bitterly.)* Yes.

CLARK: So we eliminate it! Anything else to cross out?

JAMIE: Um, "D"; "The horse is cantering by."

CLARK: Yes! Why?

JAMIE: *(Triumphant.)* Because the horse in the passage is going really fast, but a canter is a slow run! I went to horse camp.

CLARK: These tests are actually designed for people who went to horse camp. It's amazing you haven't scored higher.

JAMIE: You don't have to be so rude about this social class stuff. You have a lot more earning potential than I do, so the tables will be turned in no time.

CLARK: Will they.

JAMIE: Yes. And then you'll still hate me. Wait! Perambulate and Permanent start with the same sound!

CLARK: But the words aren't actually related —

JAMIE: Clark. Kumquat. Pineapple wedge. Sweetie. The words are unrelated — so what? They look the same! So I am expected to think they're related and dive like a lemming to my death! But, no — I just learned that anything that looks Right is Wrong! So I cross it out. Her walk is not permanent. The answer is B! Penelope is mordant. A word I don't know but checking back, it must mean . . . sarcastic! How much do I love that. So there!

(She grabs another problem set.)

CLARK: What are you doing?

JAMIE: Cross them out. Kill them off. D. E. A.

(She rapidly does another page as Clark watches.)

C. Done. I can do that. Give me another exercise.

ODDS
Hal Corley

Seriocomic
Micah, fifteen; Ilona, late teens

> *Micah suffers from "ODD" — Oppositional Defiant Disorder. Ilona is a high school senior asked by their school to mentor him. She is a rapacious power-tripper, and she wants to control Micah; mentally and sexually.*

> *The town library, a rainy fall afternoon. Ilona is subdued. Micah doodles, drums the table.*

MICAH: *I hate the smell in libraries.* They never open windows —

ILONA: Shhhh, they'll kick your shapely butt outta here.

MICAH: Yours, too, so it won't be *too* bad —

ILONA: Whisper, Babe, *whisper.* Sometimes I appreciate even the most oppressive rules. They give me something to hold onto.

MICAH: Can I *ask* you something else — but you can't *laugh.* OK? Would it be, like, totally *gay* . . . If *I* . . . *took* that . . . that "Intro to Foods" class? I walk by and I see how . . . how you can, like, actually learn to, like, *cook* shit, from scrat — *Don't look like that. Are you* laughing *at* —

ILONA: *(Over.)* — Shhh! — nobody's laughing at you! *Je*sus! *Gay?* Don't say that 'round my cousin. He's a pastry chef at this French place in Berkeley, California, and a total *player*, drives a vintage Mustang —

MICAH: Cool.

ILONA: — And who cares what the junior dickwads at school think of you? Their dads'll get 'em into colleges they're too dumb for, then they'll go play like real world Monopoly and build McMansions and ugly banks on top a' the last fuckin' cow pasture in Bumblefuck, 'Jersey. Oh God, God, *God* . . .

MICAH: — What? *What 'I say now* — ?

ILONA: — It's not you, everything isn't, I'm having one of my "shadow days." It's not a mood that's like *crisis*-generated. When it hits, I just get, like, sad to the 50th power. Know how you feel at a really tragic movie? — *Bambi?*

MICAH: Never saw it. That the one about the wise-ass rabbit?

ILONA: No, no, *deer* — well, there *is* a rabbit — but that's not my — a sad movie, where, like, when some dog gets run over, a vet has to put him down? And the vet's overwhelmingly *nice?* While some kid begs him not to, hugging the dog just before he gets the needle?

MICAH: Sorta.

ILONA: When a character's so fucked-up, you can't take the pain they're experiencing. And then it gets way worse, when someone acts, like *too kind* to them?

MICAH: But they're just made-*up*, the "vet's" a dumb actor, who, like hates dogs n' does crystal meth in his glass house on a beach.

ILONA: Whatever, on these days, it's like I'm frozen in that kinda split second.

MICAH: But why?

ILONA: The way into the library, I saw this older woman, eating an orange. Something about the way she had wrapped it up— so *conscientiously* — in a hankie, covered with teensie, faded, like, violets. Old lady flowers, I can't even *think* about her. I can just picture some room she lives in — closed-tight venetian *blinds*— where she cuts up an orange and wraps it in a perfumey keepsake from her chest of drawers that's got moth balls — moth balls are so morbid — and takes it with her when she runs all her shit errands.

MICAH: Buyin' more oranges.

ILONA: If she even has enough money to.

MICAH: She could steal 'em. Nobody in the grocery'd call the cops on some starved old person.

ILONA: But you just *sense,* she never sees another soul.

MICAH: How 'you know all that? Maybe she's gotta whole kitchen fulla oranges. And maybe she likes to go outside and eat in the fresh air, or if it's cloudy, maybe the orange color makes her happier. And maybe when you saw her, she was on her way back to meet some old dude who gave her the handkerchief, way back in, like, 1964 or something. And maybe today he'll surprise her, and kiss her wrinkly lips, and then stick his wrinkly tongue down her throat.

ILONA: Don't you dare make fun of —

MICAH: *(Over.)* I'm not! The inside of her mouth'll taste like — *he*llo! — fresh *oranges!* Which he likes, too! And maybe that's how they *share* an orange!

(Beat, Ilona breaks into a smile. Micah drops the doodling and pen, and with uncharacteristic tenderness, takes Ilona's hand. He opens it, then gently rubs his fingers across it.)

MICAH: Just 'cause people look pathetic doesn't mean they are. There's sadder stuff — sadder *things* — than a old woman with a orange and nowhere to hang out. *Sadder.* Boy. *I* know. *Lots* sadder.

PORT AUTHORITY THROW DOWN

Mike Batistick

Seriocomic
Barb and Pervez, thirties

> *Pervez is a NYC cab driver. He is Pakistani and is sick and tired of people thinking he's an Arab. Barb is a Christian missionary. Naturally, he asked her out. Talk about an odd couple . . .*

> *Scene: New York City. Early evening. At rise: Inside a taxicab in Manhattan, heading toward the Port Authority Bus Terminal. Barb, a white woman, is being driven by Pervez, a Pakistani immigrant in his thirties. News radio is playing in the background.*

BARB: Beautiful day, isn't it?

PERVEZ: Yes, lady. It is a beautiful fucking day.

BARB: God gave us a beautiful day.

PERVEZ: Do you know what would be a beautiful day?

BARB: No. What?

PERVEZ: When Israel falls.

BARB: Oh.

PERVEZ: Yes. I would like that.

BARB: Wow.

PERVEZ: Yes.

BARB: Holy Toledo.

PERVEZ: When Israel falls. It would be a good day then. You Jewish?

BARB: No.

PERVEZ: You look Jewish.

BARB: Really?

PERVEZ: Yes. Like a Jew. Do you read the Bible?

BARB: I'd like to be let out.

PERVEZ: You are going to the Port Authority. I will take you to the Port Authority. No problem. I am going there, too. You like the Bible? *(Uncomfortable pause.)* C'mon, not a hard question, it is a very popular book. *Do you like the Bible?*

BARB: I do. I like it.

PERVEZ: OK. *(Beat.)* I have a bomb in the back.

BARB: Oh, Lord.

PERVEZ: You are old American money? You have a lot of American money, right?

BARB: My father is a pool salesman from Northeastern Ohio. I'm here with my congregation —

PERVEZ: *(Cutting her off.)* I don't really have a bomb.

BARB: You don't have a bomb?

PERVEZ: No. Do you have a bomb?

BARB: No.

PERVEZ: Good. Because I have a bomb.

BARB: *(Lying.)* OK, *I* have a bomb.

PERVEZ: *(About to burst, attempting to steady his rudder.)* Ha ha ha, just kidding, lady. I am just letting out aggression. I do not really have a bomb. I do not have anything. I just have a lot of stress. Your Attorney General. He really makes people upset. Mr. Attorney General makes me have a lot of stress. He comes to my house, he takes things. How big a reader of the Bible are you? Attorney General big?

BARB: Attorney General?

PERVEZ: He is a man who reads the Bible a lot. He makes me *very* upset. Does he make you upset?

BARB: No. He doesn't make me upset.

PERVEZ: Lady, your Attorney General. He just, takes things. Do you know him? I *have* to talk to him.

BARB: I think he lives pretty far away.

PERVEZ: He takes people.

BARB: He lives in Washington.

PERVEZ: His people come to my Jersey City apartment — *pomp* — take a person right from my apartment. My brother. He took my brother, took my brother right from Journal Square.

BARB: I'm sure he didn't take your brother.

PERVEZ: Oh no? Why now do I have jihad crazy Muslims calling me up, asking me to join them?

BARB: Did your brother do something? He must have done something.

PERVEZ: He is a Port Authority newspaper salesman, he pays taxes. Now I work two jobs and got fucking pissed-off Muslims asking me to theorize with them. Because they think I now sympathize. I do not want Israel to fall. This is just a self-defense mechanism all Muslims take in times of crisis. *(Beat.)* I just got a bee in my bonnet.

BARB: You don't want Israel to fall.

PERVEZ: No.

BARB: Well, that's good to hear.

PERVEZ: Lady. Israel. You got to admit, lady, they are sort of a pain in the ass.

BARB: I don't, I think they're fine. I don't think they're a pain . . . in the fanny. Please.

PERVEZ: Admit it, they are sort of a pain in the ass to everybody. Never thought of it much before. Then, Islamists leave literature in my cab, I read the material in the pamphlet. They are a pain in my ass.

BARB: I will not talk about this *anymore.* Mr. Cab Driver, perhaps you should take these views back to your . . . kingdom.

PERVEZ: I think they, Israelis, bulldoze things too much.

BARB: Well you just think that because you are living on their land.

PERVEZ: *(Realization.) Living on their land?*

BARB: I'm about tired of hearing you complain, Mr. Cab Driver.

PERVEZ: You think I am *Palestinian?*

BARB: *(Assertive.)* One of those people, yes. *(Cab comes to a halt.)*

PERVEZ: Lady. *Pakistan.* It is very far from *Palestine.* I am not even Arab, lady. *(Taking out his clipboard, recording the fare price and final destination.)* Now I have to go to the New York City bus station and sell a stack of daily newspapers for an incarcerated brother, I do not know how to sell papers. I am a cab driver. A fucking government official took my brother. Your country is taking people from houses. I speak Urdu, I am not even fucking Arab, I have been in this country as long as anybody, stop judging, no wonder people get so upset at your nation. Everything comes out as an accusation. *(Putting the clipboard down. Beat.)* I am just tired, lady. I am just really really tired. Please. Get out. We're here. Fucking Port Authority. I am sorry. I am. Sorry that you were my "Pro-Islamist Literature" guinea pig. Get out.

BARB: Can you unlock the door?

PERVEZ: Pay me first. Then unlock the doors yourself. Fucking switch is right there.

BARB: *(Noticing it.)* Oh. *(Barb begins to dig for money in her wallet.)*

PERVEZ: I try this on you. Because you look like a tough American woman. Very rugged. Like you can take things. I had to test these theories out. But I am not fucking *Palestinian.*

BARB: *I* am not rugged.

PERVEZ: You look very rugged.

BARB: *(Handing Pervez some money.)* I know your people have your problems, and I'm trying to understand . . . your plight. But I'm coming from a very long day on the city streets. Uptown. Don't you dare call a woman *rugged.* It is very, very insulting.

PERVEZ: *(Handing Barb back her change.)* It is a bad thing to say?

BARB: *(Tipping him.)* You deserve to get your clock cleaned.

PERVEZ: I apologize. *(Beat.)* You want to have a coffee some time, you and me?

BARB: Mr. Cab Driver.

PERVEZ: Coffee. Starbuck.

BARB: Star*bucks?*

PERVEZ: *(Correcting himself.)* Star*bucks. (Beat.)* To thank you for talking.

BARB: I don't think that's a good idea.

PERVEZ: *(Hurt?)* OK. Where do people usually go when they ask people out on dates? Do they take them to coffee places? Like Star*bucks?* Just for future reference.

BARB: I don't. They could.

PERVEZ: Oh. Good. *Phew.*

BARB: *(Beat.)* Are you asking me out?

PERVEZ: No. Do . . . No, I'm . . . Sure, you want to go on a date?

BARB: I'm not really sure —

PERVEZ: If it is not too much trouble. Whatever. If you want. Starbucks. I mean, only if — this makes you uncomfortable.

BARB: No. Yes. I little bit.

PERVEZ: Forget it. I am sorry. I was just kidding 'bout Starbucks. Fuck it.

BARB: Please. Sir. Language. Your mother in Arabia I'm sure would not like to hear that potty mouth. And if you're going to take people to task simply for riding in your cab, perhaps you should take this. *(Hands him a small book.)* And learn a little charity.

PERVEZ: What are you giving me?

BARB: Oh, I'm supposed to hand this out. My minister at the Assembly of God said to give this to people. If you want to get coffee, leave a message there and I will call you back if I can. There is a number inside.

PERVEZ: What is it?

BARB: I just gave you a Bible.

PERVEZ: A Bible?

BARB: A portable Bible. For your pocket.

PERVEZ: *(Admiring it.)* A portable Bible. For your pocket. *(Beat.)* OK. thank you. Miss, I have never been on an American date. So I can prepare. What things would you want to talk about when we go out on this date?

BARB: Scripture.

PERVEZ: What is your name?

BARB: Barb.

PERVEZ: *Barb.*

BARB: Barb Heckerd. What is your name?

PERVEZ: Pervez.

BARB: Mr. Pervez. It is a pleasure to meet you. It's nice to see you immigrants working so hard. I hope you find your brother.

PERVEZ: Thank you. *(Barb exits, stepping out of the car. Baffled, thumbing through the Bible.)* Scripture? What the fuck is a scripture?

PORT AUTHORITY THROW DOWN
Mike Batistick

Seriocomic
Barb and Pervez, thirties

> *Pervez is a NYC cab driver. He is Pakistani and is sick and tired of
> people thinking he's an Arab. Barb is a Christian missionary.
> Naturally, he asked her out. Here, they are having coffee. Talk
> about an odd couple . . .*

> *Pervez and Barb having coffee in the cab.*

BARB: Well, one day very soon, Pervez, they say you might come to my
house and it will be empty. Jesus is going to come down to Earth
and he's going to take all the good Christians like me and my family — and hopefully you — up with Him to heaven to sit at His
table. And everyone else, like *maybe* you if you don't come aboard in
time, will be stuck here. Condemned to eternity in hell. While all
the Christians will be sitting next to Jesus in Heaven.

PERVEZ: *(Clarifying.)* So all the *(Struggling for the correct language.)* "hea-
thens" will die. And you, the Christians, will be taken up to heaven
by "The Rapture."

BARB: Precisely. See. You're catching on.

PERVEZ: This "End of Days" scenario. OK. It is a very strange concept.

BARB: I know. But nobody said the Lord was easy.

PERVEZ: No.

BARB: So, Pervez.

PERVEZ: What?

BARB: I think if you came to Bible class, you might enjoy it.

PERVEZ: Oh. *(Changing the subject.)* Perhaps we can talk about the
impending American World Series.

BARB: OK.

PERVEZ: I predict it will be the Anaheim Angels and the San Francisco Giants in the annual seven-game slugfest. The Yankees and the New York Metropolitans, I do not think these two franchises will make it to the championship.

BARB: OK. So you like baseball? Since you got here?

PERVEZ: I am not a big fan yet but I have a feeling I will be one soon. However it is a very nice thing to just bring up at times. Although it would be easier to bring up cricket, though.

BARB: Cricket?

PERVEZ: It is a sport. Like baseball. In Pakistan, I know more about it.

BARB: A cricket is a bug here.

PERVEZ: I know.

BARB: You're real cute, Pervez.

PERVEZ: Thank you. *(Looking at his coffee cup.)* Does everyone drink this crap?

BARB: Yes.

PERVEZ: I think it is nasty.

BARB: You shoulda seen the first gourmet coffee chain in Akron, Ohio. Whoa, boy. Hot cakes.

PERVEZ: Akron. What an interesting town name.

BARB: Cleveland's the real *New York* in those parts. It's got the baseball team and the football team. Akron's just "The Former Rubber Capital of the World." Good thing it's still got pools to install. For my daddy. Lot more above grounds now, however. It's cheaper, y'know. Above grounds.

PERVEZ: If my mother knew I was sitting here with a pretty Christian white woman, I think she would shit.

BARB: My minister sent me out here to convert people, thinking it was the end of the world. But it sure doesn't feel like that's happening anymore, does it?

PERVEZ: No. Not really.

BARB: No. It doesn't.

PERVEZ: Except for all the dead people. In the papers. Every day. And for the fact that my brother was taken. *(Beat.)* So will you return to Akron then?

BARB: I don't know. The mission I'm staying at here is a little strange. Sometimes New York can be very loud.

PERVEZ: This city can be loud. And obtrusive. I agree. But things will be fine, I think. I just need to find my brother.

BARB: I think you will find him.

PERVEZ: Can you. Talk to somebody?

BARB: Wait. What?

PERVEZ: Can you talk to somebody? To see if he is OK?

BARB: What are you talking about?

PERVEZ: Y'know. Call somebody up. You are white.

BARB: What? Do you, who do you think I am?

PERVEZ: We need to talk to somebody.

BARB: We could write a Congressman. But that might take a while.

PERVEZ: Like, how long?

BARB: Months. It depends on how many letters you write him and how crazy you sound.

PERVEZ: We would not sound crazy.

BARB: Oh, I know.

PERVEZ: I drove by my home in Jersey City six days ago only to see the Federal Bureau of Investigations men outside my house. I have no choice but drive on, to leave my brother and to let my cat rot in that house. He is a good cat, too. Surely all my neighbors will think that I, too, was incarcerated. Barb. Nawaz is a very nice guy. He's just overweight. We are not crazy.

BARB: Nawaz?

PERVEZ: Nawaz. His name is Nawaz.

BARB: That sounds like a nice name.

PERVEZ: It is. In Pakistan, everything is Allah and power and fighting. In Jersey City, it is not like that. It *was* not like that. Every place in the world feels like exactly the same place to me right now. It really sucks.

BARB: I'm sorry. It *sucks.*

PERVEZ: It's OK. It does not suck that bad sitting next to you, however.

BARB: Thank you Pervez. Likewise. *(Beat.)* Pervez?

PERVEZ: Yes?

BARB: Nothing.

PERVEZ: What?

BARB: *(Beat.)* For the first time since I got here. To New York City. I feel a little God.

PERVEZ: You do?

BARB: Yes. Between us.

PERVEZ: What's he feel like?

BARB: He's a warm feeling. Here in this part of the country, I don't feel like He is here that often.

PERVEZ: I don't feel like he is around much here, either.

BARB: He's supposed to be everywhere.

PERVEZ: Barb. Your father, the pool salesman, how big is your pool that he has installed in your backyard?

BARB: Oh. *We* don't have one. No. I've just swum in one.

PERVEZ: Oh.

BARB: Pools are very expensive, Pervez. When you wanna swim in one, in my family you gotta go over to a friend's home.

PERVEZ: A rich friend's home.

BARB: Yeah. Somebody rich.

PERVEZ: I hope you do not return to Akron. Perhaps I could build a pool for you here.

BARB: I don't need a pool.

PERVEZ: Do you not need your Akron then either?

BARB: I don't know. I really don't know. I don't know if I can stay here.

PERVEZ: Sometimes I think the very same thing.

SCHOOL OF THE AMERICAS

José Rivera

Dramatic
Che, thirty-nine; Julia, twenties

> *Che Guevara has been captured in Bolivia and imprisoned in a village. His jail is a dilapidated shack which is the village's only school. Julia, the teacher, has been allowed by Che's jailers to keep him company.*

CHE: Do you know what Ramos plans to do with me?

JULIA: No — I just — I think of those idiots out there —

CHE: What about you? Are you married? Where's your family?

JULIA: My family is my sister and me. She's sick. Most foods disagree with her. And there are so many shortages here, she's malnourished. I take care of her. There's no one else. No husband, no man.

CHE: You're still young and very . . . well, not all that unattractive . . . there's no reason for you to be alone.

JULIA: Yes, well, my work doesn't leave a lot of room for romance. No matter what my sister thinks. She's always making fun of me for being: *(Imitating Lucila.)* "A pathetic, romantic fool."

CHE: Imagine that.

JULIA: This is a world where life can get so small and simple. Men raise pigs and grow kinoa and potatoes. There's birth and death and the little, unimportant things that happen in between.

CHE: Yet those "little things" are everything, don't you think?
(Julia can't help but laugh.)

JULIA: You're a hypocrite, you know that?

CHE: Are you actually laughing at me?

JULIA: Those "little things," Che . . . I mean, Mr. —

CHE: Che. It's Che. Actually it's *el* Che, but you can drop the *"el"* if you wish.

JULIA: Weren't they the things you had before you came here? A wife, her smile, her words, your children's voice in the morning . . . you *had* them, they were *yours*. But they weren't enough for you. You wanted . . .

CHE: To change everything and everyone around me.

JULIA: Yes, the whole crazy world. I'm sorry. I don't mean to criticize you.

CHE: I can take criticism.

JULIA: I'm sure you can, but I'm in no position to judge you.

CHE: Leaders must be judged.

JULIA: I guess I don't understand you, and, I don't know, I guess if it was me and I had your life, I would've been happy and I would've stayed home to savor all the good things that were coming to me, the things I earned from my hard work.

CHE: Such as?

JULIA: My children's love. A love that can change the world — *(Che laughs.)*

CHE: "A love that can change the world!" That's brilliant!

JULIA: — the devotion and trust of my spouse. The years as they add up on my children's faces. The world reflected in their eyes. A family that's like a coat you spread around your body and nothing can harm you. Not disease or sadness or old age. Someone to say your name in a voice no one else in the world uses.

CHE: Yes, you must drive your sister absolutely crazy.

JULIA: It would be nice if you would take what I say seriously.

CHE: I bet you've been thinking this romantic nonsense all your life.

JULIA: Yes, well, La Higuera can be a lonely place.

CHE: Yet you've never left.

JULIA: I didn't see a reason.

CHE: Funny. I've done nothing but leave.

JULIA: You're a man, you're allowed.

CHE: Bullshit. You could've left. In Cuba, many women besides Aleida left the safety of their homes to fight in the Sierra Maestra.

JULIA: The world isn't Cuba.

CHE: Well, it should be. And someday it will be. And schools like this won't exist. Every place will have new modern schools, with actual floors, and large windows, and the latest textbooks, and not just one sorry, burned-out teacher who can't conjugate —

JULIA: I can too!

CHE: — but an army of dedicated teachers, working around the clock — and not only will they educate the children, they will educate the *family*. It's pointless to bring a child to school only to send them home to ignorance and superstition. Learning must happen *every minute*. Mothers and fathers must be educated and must be able to teach each other, their children, and *every* child in the village. Can you imagine? A world of constant learning . . . every person will simultaneously be teacher and student . . .

(Che stops — a stabbing pain in his stomach doubles him over. Though he does his best not to cry out, the pain is too great to keep inside.)
(Che coughs, spits up blood.)
(Julia watches, alarmed, unable to help him, torn between wanting to go to him and calling out for help.)
(Che's intense pain continues through the scene . . .)

JULIA: I can't believe they let you lie here without —

CHE: I'm alright — it'll pass —

JULIA: I can call the Lieutenant —

CHE: I'd rather vomit my own lungs!

JULIA: It's disgusting what they're doing to you., We're supposed to be a God-fearing, Christian nation —

CHE: It's been my experience the more a country invokes the name of God the more likely they are to torture and destroy their own and other people. You can't be naive about the intentions of your government. Especially since you don't really have a government.

JULIA: Are you sure you're OK . . . ?

(Che doesn't want to surrender to the terrible pain.)

CHE: Your government has a government. Did you know that? And it's this greater government which really controls what happens in this school. Who do you think your friend Lieutenant Ramos works for?

(Julia is still pre-occupied with his pain.)

JULIA: Please don't call him my friend.

CHE: North Americans train the specialists and mercenaries who hunted me down. North Americans pay Ramos to interrogate me and photograph my journal and torture my companions. North Americans shove money up the ass of your President Barrientos and force the right words to come out of his mouth.

(Julia looks at Che — a little shocked over his last metaphor.)

(Che can see his language has offended her.)

Now what is it?

JULIA: I'm sorry — I don't like — I know you're a soldier —

CHE: My language.

JULIA: Yes, your language. I'm sorry — I —

CHE: The North Americans fuck Barrientos up the ass in order to make the cocksucking sell-out do their bidding. *That* language?

JULIA: Oh God — that's really bad —

(Julia crosses herself.)

CHE: Don't do that.

JULIA: Do what?

CHE: Cross yourself.

JULIA: Why not?

CHE: It's inane. It does nothing but make you look like an ignorant ape.

JULIA: I'm sorry — but I will cross myself as often as I need to —

CHE: To ward off the evil of evil language?

JULIA: Because it puts me closer to God —

CHE: *Ass* —!

(Julia crosses herself.)

JULIA: Stop it.

CHE: *Fucking the ass* —!

(Julia crosses herself.)

JULIA: Oh God!

CHE: *Big fat, gross tits covered in the semen of the local priest!*

(Julia crosses herself.)

JULIA: My God, I can't believe this! You're going to burn in hell for this!

(Che tries not to laugh.)

(Julia laughs despite herself and crosses herself again.)

CHE: Really? For how long?

JULIA: Eternity!

CHE: Not long enough! *Lyndon Johnson likes to fuck the Pope up his holy butt-hole with a twelve inch crucifix —*!

JULIA: Enough! Enough! Please!

(Julia stands, laughing, unable to look at him.)

SPAIN
Jim Knabel

Comic

Barbara, late twenties to early thirties; Conquistador, the same

> *Barbara has walked into her living room and found a sixteenth*
> *Century Spanish Conquistador sitting on her sofa. Is he real or is he*
> *a figment of her imagination?*

BARBARA: What are you, really?

CONQUISTADOR: What do you believe?

BARBARA: I don't know what to think.

CONQUISTADOR: Do not think.

BARBARA: Who do you think I am?

CONQUISTADOR: I am not thinking.

BARBARA: A woman in man's clothing? A vision?

CONQUISTADOR: Yes.

BARBARA: Which story is true?

CONQUISTADOR: Both.

> *(Conquistador stands in his Sixteenth Century underwear. Barbara*
> *motions for him to sit on the floor by the table. She pulls a bottle of*
> *whiskey out from under the table, drinks from it. He drinks. She*
> *drinks. He drinks.)*
> *. . . (She reaches under the table and pulls out a large travel book. She*
> *opens it and shows it to Conquistador.)*

BARBARA: It's been my fantasy for a long time.

CONQUISTADOR: Spain.

BARBARA: I wanted to go there with John. I wanted that to be the place
where we found love again. I wanted a country to love.

CONQUISTADOR: You want love.

BARBARA: Wanted.

CONQUISTADOR: And now?

BARBARA: Tell me what it feels like to kill someone.

CONQUISTADOR: You already know.

BARBARA: A whole civilization. What is that like?

CONQUISTADOR: It is like nothing else.

BARBARA: It makes you feel strong.

CONQUISTADOR: Yes.

BARBARA: Because they can't defend themselves against your weapons.

CONQUISTADOR: Yes.

BARBARA: And you can do anything you want with them?

CONQUISTADOR: Yes.

    (Barbara drinks.)

BARBARA: Cut off their heads.

CONQUISTADOR: Of course.

BARBARA: Disembowel them.

CONQUISTADOR: Certainly.

BARBARA: Cut off their balls.

CONQUISTADOR: Occasionally.

BARBARA: You ride into town with your men, in your armor; you all stink like horses . . .

CONQUISTADOR: Horses, oh yes!

BARBARA: The villagers stare up at you terrified, helpless, you don't even see them as human . . .

CONQUISTADOR: Villagers?

BARBARA: The weak, the peasants . . .

CONQUISTADOR: Peasants, pthuh . . .

BARBARA: Then what?

CONQUISTADOR: Kill the peasants!

BARBARA: Yes! You hit your heels on your horse and ride through them, swooping your sword, hacking, slashing . . .

CONQUISTADOR: *(Suggesting.)* Chopping?

BARBARA: Chopping up and down!
    You take up a fiery lance, you hurl it through the air, it soars, fire trailing, down into the hut where the men hold ceremonies; it bursts into flames.

CONQUISTADOR: Many, many flames!

BARBARA: You burn it all down, you leave nothing standing. The dirt roads run muddy with blood.

CONQUISTADOR: Muddy blood.

BARBARA: You drink the blood, your mouth is red, you run, screaming
battle cries, killing everything in your path, even your own men,
your lust consumes you.

CONQUISTADOR: You are very good at this.

BARBARA: You burn with death and pain, painless pain because you feel
nothing but overpowering joy, you spin your arms and wave your
sword and stand on top off all the bodies, like a mountain, you
stand on top and breathe in the smell of torn-out flesh!
(Conquistador drinks.)

CONQUISTADOR: Yes, all that. I do that.

This drink is good. What is it?

BARBARA: Whiskey.

John drank it, his bottle.

BARBARA: *(Gleefully, with him.)* Why do I still keep it?

CONQUISTADOR: *(As before with the portrait.)* Why do you still keep it?
(She takes another swig and hurls it offstage. Crash! They laugh.)

BARBARA: I could destroy everything.

The couch. We bought it together.
*(She goes to the couch and tears into the pillows, hurling them, violent
and crazy. Conquistador helps some, but is no match for her fury.)*
What else? More pictures? I have more pictures. Dishes? The sheets?
His smell still on them. Everything here we had together, I could
destroy everything!

CONQUISTADOR: You are amazing.

BARBARA: I could destroy, myself, I could destroy . . . I could . . .
(She flops down on the remains of the couch.)
Too much, too fast. Spinning.

CONQUISTADOR: Spinning. Yes, spinning your arms.

BARBARA: Room spinning.

Can't look.

Too much…
(She collapses.)

CONQUISTADOR: Barbara?

SPAIN
Jim Knabel

Comic
Barbara, late twenties to early thirties; Conquistador, the same

Here, Barbara goes to Spain (she's always dreamed of going there) with a Spanish Conquistador who appeared in her living room, sitting on her sofa, wearing his helmet and armor.

CONQUISTADOR: Careful. It is a great distance down from this cliff.

BARBARA: Where are we going?

CONQUISTADOR: To the valley. Over that stream. Through those woods.

BARBARA: What is our destination?

CONQUISTADOR: My home.

BARBARA: Your house.

CONQUISTADOR: We must get there before dark.

BARBARA: What happens after dark?

CONQUISTADOR: Wolves.

BARBARA: It's strange. You're nothing like you were, but it's still you.

CONQUISTADOR: We will also have to pass through a waterfall. Up ahead, beyond that ridge.

BARBARA: Do I seem different?

CONQUISTADOR: It is always hard to understand you.

BARBARA: Other than that.

CONQUISTADOR: Yes. You keep changing.

BARBARA: Are you sad that you aren't a Conquistador anymore?

CONQUISTADOR: A little. I am glad we could meet again.

BARBARA: Oh? Why is that?

CONQUISTADOR: You help me to understand myself.

BARBARA: Oh.

CONQUISTADOR: Come. We are nearly to the waterfall.

BARBARA: This is where you live?

CONQUISTADOR: Yes.

(Beat.)

BARBARA: I like it.

CONQUISTADOR: It is not soft like your house.

BARBARA: That's fine.

CONQUISTADOR: Would you like to sit?

(Conquistador gestures. Barbara sits. She looks at him, he looks at her.)
Are you thirsty?

BARBARA: Yes.

CONQUISTADOR: Wait here.

(Conquistador disappears. She is alone.)

BARBARA: *(Calling for him.)* El Tigre? Pepe?

(Conquistador appears with two clay cups full of mead and a rolled-up piece of parchment. He sets everything down and sits.)

CONQUISTADOR: I have something to show you.

(Conquistador unrolls the parchment. It is a drawing of a conquistador on horseback.)

BARBARA: A Conquistador. Did you draw that?

CONQUISTADOR: No. It was given to me. Do you want to hear the story?

BARBARA: Is it true? Nevermind, that doesn't even matter. Tell me the story.

CONQUISTADOR: I was out in the fields.

BARBARA: The lush green countryside.

CONQUISTADOR: The fields of the farm. It was planting season.

BARBARA: Of course.

CONQUISTADOR: A shadow fell over me while I bent to the earth. I looked up to see a man dressed as I have never seen a man dressed. I asked him who he was. I asked him where he was from? He held out this parchment for me to take. I stood and unrolled it. The sun glowed brown off the earth. I saw this. What is this? And he told me what that meant. He spoke of the New World. Of Savages. Of noble knights on horseback claiming the land from a people destined to be conquered. Of their ladies and their power. I asked him if he was one of them. And then the sun grew big in the sky and his white clothes blinded my eyes. When I could see again, he was gone. I was left alone in the fields with this. When I returned home that night, I looked at it again. I studied it for hours. Sometimes I could hear the sound in my head of horses' hoofs stomping or of victory cries. I could hear fire crackling. I smelled smoke. And when I put my face close, I could see a shape carefully drawn on the helmet.

BARBARA: A tiger.

CONQUISTADOR: Yes.

BARBARA: I used to sit at my desk at work and make lists of cities. Spanish cities. Barcelona, Madrid, San Sebastían: I looked them up, collected pictures. I made a book of the pictures. The cathedrals, the rolling golden hills, people laughing and drinking, playing guitars, dancing flamenco, always lit by fire all around them; people living unafraid of anything, so full of passion and life and —

CONQUISTADOR: Duende!

BARBARA: Duende.

CONQUISTADOR: Burning coals.

BARBARA: Boiling blood.

CONQUISTADOR: Purpose.

BARBARA: Action.

CONQUISTADOR: In my guts.

BARBARA: Down my spine.

CONQUISTADOR: In my center.

BARBARA: In my soul.

> *(Pause.)*

BARBARA: *(Continued.)* You said I helped you understand yourself. What did you mean?

> How did I help you?

CONQUISTADOR: You were a better Conquistador than I ever could be.

> You made me remember my true self.

> That is who I am now.

BARBARA: *(They drink.)* You wanted to sleep with me. Was that as the Conquistador or as you?

> *(Silence.)*

> Don't be embarrassed.

CONQUISTADOR: I grew excited when I touched you.

BARBARA: Obviously. It excited me a little, too.

CONQUISTADOR: Truly?

BARBARA: A little. It also disturbed me. I haven't been touched by a man other than my husband in many years. And when he touched me, it wasn't the way that you touched me. Even though his hands were warm and yours were cold.

CONQUISTADOR: I have never been so bold with a woman.

BARBARA: Have you ever been with a woman?

(Silence.)

BARBARA: *(Continued.)* It's all right.

This drink is good. What is it?

CONQUISTADOR: Mead.

BARBARA: You made it yourself, didn't you?

CONQUISTADOR: Yes.

(Barbara smiles.)

What is it? Why are you smiling?

BARBARA: I really like you.

(Silence. Barbara leans across and kisses Conquistador gently on the lips. She pulls back.)

Have you ever felt that?

(He bows his head.)

Did it feel good?

CONQUISTADOR: Yes.

BARBARA: You're shivering.

Close your eyes.

(He does. She kisses him again, holding him to her.)

(Diversion appears in a separate space in her Flamenco dress, slipping it off as she talks. Underneath she wears a simple white slip. Her tone reflects this.)

Scratchy face.

CONQUISTADOR: What?

BARBARA: Your beard. Scratchy face. It's nice.

CONQUISTADOR: Thank you.

BARBARA: Do you know what to do next?

CONQUISTADOR: Next?

BARBARA: Touch me the way you touched me before.

SUGGESTIBILITY

Jon Klein

Dramatic
Kenneth and Shawn, thirties

> *Kenneth and Shawn are hotshots working for a financial institu-*
> *tion. Another man (Chad) is close to Shawn, but she is more inter-*
> *ested in the mysterious Kenneth.*

KENNETH: Is there . . . pardon me if I'm getting too personal . . .

SHAWN: Feel free. That's the whole point of this.

KENNETH: You and Chad . . .

SHAWN: What?

KENNETH: He seems very . . . interested.

SHAWN: Oh.

KENNETH: In you.

SHAWN: Chad and I have a long-standing . . . I hesitate to call it a relationship . . . more of a codependent revulsion.

KENNETH: I . . . see.

SHAWN: Sorry. I don't mean to be obtuse. Or to be so obtuse as to use
words like "obtuse."

KENNETH: So you and Chad . . .

SHAWN: Are just friends. Not to worry.

KENNETH: You're sure about his end of it? Maybe he's just reluctant to
tell you his feelings.

SHAWN: That will be the day.

KENNETH: Sometimes it's hard to know what's going on.

SHAWN: Then allow me to be straightforward. *(She leans over and kisses
him lightly on the lips.)* Or maybe just forward. . .

KENNETH: Whichever it was . . . it was very nice.

SHAWN: Thank you. There are many variations.

KENNETH: It's just . . . I'm not a good candidate for this.

SHAWN: This? What do you call this?

KENNETH: Whatever you . . . think this is.

SHAWN: Well, so far . . . not much.

KENNETH: I'm sorry.

SHAWN: So what's the problem? You're not attracted to me?

KENNETH: God, yes. You're an extremely beautiful woman. Way out of my league.

SHAWN: I intimidate you?

KENNETH: Not at all.

SHAWN: I bore you?

KENNETH: Please — it's not you at all. It's me.

SHAWN: So it's the other woman.

KENNETH: No.

SHAWN: Assuming she *is* a woman.

KENNETH: She said she was.

SHAWN: *Said* she was? What does that mean? She's a transsexual?

KENNETH: Please. Let me explain. *(He takes a sip from her drink, then hands it back to her.)* Here's the problem — I don't know what love is.

SHAWN: So fucking what? Neither do I. No one does. Welcome to the human race.

KENNETH: But you know what it feels like.

SHAWN: Well, yeah. I've been there once or twice.

KENNETH: I never have.

SHAWN: Oh. Well, there are many kinds of love, Kenneth. It doesn't always have to be romantic. How about your parents?

KENNETH: Oh, they went through the motions, I suppose. But they really didn't notice I was there, most of the time.

SHAWN: It might have felt that way —

KENNETH: No. It *was* that way. So I made up imaginary creatures. Monsters. Pirates. Alternate parents. They were easier to talk to.

SHAWN: You were just lonely. And longing for love.

KENNETH: See, that makes no sense to me. It's like longing for Thai food when you've never tasted it. I was like some kind of jungle boy, raised by wolves.

SHAWN: Actually, wolves are very affectionate.

KENNETH: Really. I didn't know that. Where was I?

SHAWN: In the jungle.

KENNETH: Oh, right. Childhood. Then high school. Where I watched everyone go through their first romances, crushes and heartbreaks. From the outside. Like some . . . cultural anthropologist.

SHAWN: Big deal. You managed to avoid the worst part of adolescence. You were lucky.

KENNETH: I didn't feel lucky. I felt stupid. So I started reading up on the subject.

SHAWN: What subject? You mean —

KENNETH: This thing called love. I went on a self-taught, remedial course. I read Keats, Shelley, Byron, all the Romantic poets. Shakespeare, Plato, Kierkegaard, Leo Buscaglia. Romantic films — *Casablanca, Wuthering Heights, Love Story.* My favorite was *Vertigo.*

SHAWN: *Vertigo?* That's a little unhealthy, don't you think?

KENNETH: I couldn't make those distinctions. I still couldn't figure out what I was expected to feel. Other than the brief, temporary satisfaction of sexual release. At first I confused *that* for love. I bet you never made *that* mistake.

SHAWN: Well . . . Hey. We're not here to talk about me.

KENNETH: Then suddenly, without any warning, it happened.

SHAWN: Thank God. I've been waiting for the juicy part.

KENNETH: It's also . . . the hardest part. How do I explain this to you? You remember how I said I never actually *saw* her? In person?

SHAWN: Yes . . .

KENNETH: We met on the Internet.

(Pause.)

SHAWN: Oh no.

KENNETH: I know how it sounds . . .

SHAWN: In what, a chat room?

KENNETH: That's out of date. Now it's called "social software."

SHAWN: I can't believe . . . didn't you *know* any better? Than to trust some . . . figment of somebody else's imagination? Do you know how removed that is from reality?

KENNETH: Oh yes. That was the part I liked the most.

SHAWN: Oh my God.

KENNETH: Her moniker was "Ursula." She worked as a waitress in a Bay Area cafe.

SHAWN: How ambitious.

KENNETH: It was a whole new experience for me. My heart started to beat more quickly just by turning on the computer. I couldn't wait to sign on.

SHAWN: With a fantasy!

KENNETH: I know. *(Pause.)* Until she made it real. Too real.

SHAWN: What happened?

KENNETH: She started to suggest we meet in person.

SHAWN: Oh. Well, that's only natural.

KENNETH: Not for me.

SHAWN: Why? Too scared?

KENNETH: No. Too . . . disappointed. I liked things the way they were.

SHAWN: Another movie title.

KENNETH: It was never the same after that. And she could tell how my tone changed. Without ever knowing why. All she knew was that I seemed more distant —

SHAWN: As though that's even *possible* —

KENNETH: I knew it wasn't real. But I couldn't help it. I preferred my own version.

SHAWN: The poor girl.

KENNETH: And there it is. Now she's the one who gets your sympathy. Not me.

SHAWN: Well, I suppose . . .

KENNETH: See what I mean, Shawn. I'm not the man for you. It's better to leave me alone. All I do is cause damage. That's why I quit my job and fled. I had to get as far away as possible.

SHAWN: But why here?

KENNETH: No particular reason. The furthest location to accept my resume, I suppose.

SHAWN: This is utterly absurd. Don't you ever wonder what would have happened if you met her?

KENNETH: All the time. But it's too late.

SHAWN: It's never too late. It might be worth the try.

KENNETH: I can't. *(Pause.)* She's dead.

SHAWN: My God, Kenneth. How do you know?

KENNETH: I killed her. *(He sips on his drink.)*

SCENES FOR ONE MAN AND ONE WOMAN 85

SUGGESTIBILITY
Jon Klein

Dramatic
Chad and Shawn, thirties

> *Chad and Shawn work at a top financial institution. They have a love/hate relationship.*

> *The office cubicle. Shawn is working at the computer while Chad sits on the corner of the desk.*

CHAD: Friday night.

SHAWN: No.

CHAD: Saturday night.

SHAWN: Why don't you ever take "no" for an answer?

CHAD: "No" isn't an answer. It's a reply. But it doesn't answer anything.

SHAWN: All right, here's your answer. Three answers. One. Because after ten or twenty destructive relationships, I've learned that it would be simpler just to hit myself in the head with the claw end of a hammer. Two. Because I'm apparently looking for a different species of male than the ones found on this particular planet. And three. Because the next time I decide to throw caution to the wind, my very last choice for a date would be a sexually aggressive, verbally abusive, high-maintenance mass of hostility like you.
(Pause.)

CHAD: You're secretly attracted to me, aren't you?

SHAWN: I wonder what you're really like, Chad.
Under all the pretense.

CHAD: You think I'm pretending? To be what?

SHAWN: I'm not sure. But I don't think it's human.

CHAD: What would you like me to be?

SHAWN: I'm curious about what makes you so insecure that you have to overcompensate.

CHAD: What are you talking about? I'm completely relaxed.

SHAWN: You're as relaxed as a used car dealer. And about as subtle.

CHAD: Is it wrong to go after the things you want?

SHAWN: In your case, yes.

CHAD: OK. I'll leave you alone.

SHAWN: No you won't.

CHAD: Why do you hate me?

SHAWN: I don't hate you, Chad. I don't even know you. You won't allow it. You've got this elaborate charade of personality all worked out, to take the place of something more genuine. Something that must scare you pretty badly. I wonder what it is.

CHAD: I've got nothing to hide.

SHAWN: Of course you do. We all do. But you're hiding the wrong part. Most people keep their dark and twisted sides under wraps. Out of sight. Not you. You push it right up front where everyone gapes at it in horror.

CHAD: Now you're just insulting me.

SHAWN: I wish I knew whatever caused all this.

CHAD: Whoever.

SHAWN: Whomever. A woman. Of course. What was her name?

CHAD: Let's see. Should I do this alphabetically? There was Alice. And Barbara.

SHAWN: This is a lot of anger for one man to handle.

CHAD: And Cynthia. And Darlene. And Erin. And —

SHAWN: You're actually going to come up with twenty-six.

CHAD: In the first round.

SHAWN: Which one is your mother?

CHAD: They all are. Isn't that what you're thinking?

SHAWN: Didn't occur to me.

CHAD: Tell me something. What qualifies you to judge me?

SHAWN: You're right. I apologize. After all, I have my own list of names.

CHAD: Then why not give me a chance?

SHAWN: Look, Chad. It's one thing to step in front of an approaching train. That's being . . . oblivious, I guess. Unaware. But to see the train coming first, and then to take the same step — that's either being stupid or suicidal. Either way — no thanks.

CHAD: What if I love you?

(She stifles a laugh.)

SHAWN: Oh, God. And you said you were serious.

CHAD: I am.

SHAWN: Let's not do this, Chad.

CHAD: Do what?

SHAWN: Use words.

CHAD: Words?

SHAWN: Words like "love".

CHAD: It's not just a word.

SHAWN: Yes it is. That's my point exactly. It's *never* more than just a word.

CHAD: And you accuse *me* of being cynical.

SHAWN: Words. Vows of passion, promises of faithfulness, endless proclamations of eternal devotion. Just words. Love is a dead language. Like Latin.

CHAD: So you don't believe in love.

SHAWN: I believe in action. In the form of personal sacrifice. Can you possibly know what that means?

(Pause. She burns her gaze into his face.)

CHAD: I think so.

SHAWN: I don't think you do. You should see the expression on your face right now. Like a cow staring at a passing car.

CHAD: Then explain.

SHAWN: Maybe later.

Scenes for Two Men

AREA OF RESCUE

Laura Eason

Dramatic
Gordon, thirties; Ivo, twenty-three

> *Gordon's wife has recently died in a ferry-boat accident; but Gordon has reason to believe this was no accident. Here he is asking Ivo, the boyfriend of his step-daughter, what he may or may not know about his wife's death.*

IVO: Gordon, I'd like to start with you, if I may.

GORDON: Of course.

IVO: Can you tell me about the accident from your point of view?

GORDON: *(After a moment.)* We were on the ferry and the weather was bad. Lily was standing out on the deck. I tried to get her to go in, but you know how she is, very stubborn. I was holding her arm, which was wet and slippery from the spray. The boat lurched suddenly and she slipped over. I tried to hold her hand with my hand, but I couldn't. I knew that the water was very dangerous so I threw in the life ring, so I'd have something to hold onto in the water and dove in. But I couldn't find her. She had that heavy coat on —

[RUTH: The swing coat.]

GORDON: It must have been so heavy in the water. It was only a few seconds, even though it felt like forever. I must have been yelling because one of the crew men was on the deck right after I jumped in. The storm passed quickly and we looked and looked but we couldn't find her.

IVO: And they found her body the next day.

GORDON: Yes.

IVO: I read the report from the doctor that examined her.

GORDON: Yes?

IVO: Did you know she was pregnant?

GORDON: Yes, yes I did.

IVO: But you hadn't made it public knowledge?

GORDON: No. *(After a moment.)* We've had a lot of problems over the years. We just wanted to wait to make sure everything was going to be alright.

IVO: And was it alright?

GORDON: Um, no. It wasn't.

IVO: Had you been to see Doctor Edvan last week?

GORDON: Yes.

IVO: Well, when we spoke with him —

GORDON: You spoke to him?

IVO: Yes. He told me something. Do you know what he might have told me?

GORDON: I assume he told you that our baby had died.

IVO: Yes, he did. And I'm sorry about that.

GORDON: Thank you.

IVO: And so was he.

GORDON: Yes. He was very compassionate.

IVO: He said she was five months along?

GORDON: Yes, five months.

IVO: So, what was the procedure?

GORDON: He didn't tell you?

IVO: I'd like for you to tell me what you understood it to be.

GORDON: They did a bunch of tests to make sure Lily was alright and then we made a birth appointment. *(Explaining.)* They induce you and the pregnancy is concluded that way.

IVO: I imagine that would be very difficult.

GORDON: Yes, well . . .

IVO: So, you scheduled an appointment?

GORDON: Yes. We saw Doctor Edvan on a Tuesday and the next birth appointment he had was the following Wednesday.

IVO: Over a week?

GORDON: He's very busy, as I'm sure you know.

IVO: That must have been difficult.

GORDON: We spent a lot of time in "rumination and reflection."

IVO: I'm sure you did.

GORDON: It always helped Lily.

IVO: But not you?

GORDON: Honestly, no. Not as much.

IVO: So, Friday came.

GORDON: Yes. Friday.

IVO: And what happened?

GORDON: Well, the night before Lily was talking, the doctor probably told you about the test?

IVO: Yes.

GORDON: So, you know that even if the child had lived, it would have had some significant problems.

IVO: Physical and mental problems.

GORDON: Yes. Both. Significant.

IVO: But still a "face of the faith" — as valued as any.

[RUTH: Of course.]

IVO: As it has been told.

(Ivo performs the ritualistic gesture, moving his hand from his mouth to his heart with an open flat hand. Mia and Ruth both mimic the gesture completely. Gordon does the gesture as well, but less fully. Aleeah does not do the gesture.)

IVO: So, you and Lily were talking . . . ?

GORDON: We were talking. And, as you know, across the water, there is the Children's Hospital, for children with difficulties. She said she wanted to go and visit them. I have no other explanations. She just wanted to see the children there.

IVO: Do you know why?

GORDON: Most of those children have been left in the care of the state. I think that maybe she imagined bringing one of them home.

IVO: Really?

GORDON: I don't know for sure, she didn't say that. But . . . she was so happy to have another child — and was ready for whatever that child was going to be.

IVO: Why didn't you ever adopt?

GORDON: What?

IVO: You only have Hedy. Just one.

GORDON: We had many problems.

IVO: And you didn't want to adopt?

GORDON: It's not that we didn't want to . . . Lily just wanted to have our own. I don't know.

IVO: So, you got on the ferry to go to the Children's Hospital. At what time?

GORDON: It was 10 A.M.

IVO: Were there a lot of passengers on the ferry?

GORDON: Hardly any.

IVO: Not a busy time.

GORDON: No.

IVO: And how was Lily?

GORDON: How was she?

IVO: What was her state of mind?

GORDON: She was alright. I mean she was upset about the baby, but she was alright.

IVO: The Captain said she seemed nervous.

GORDON: Oh?

IVO: He said she was nervous. And that it reminded him of other women he sees on the ferry, who usually ride at the quiet time of day.

GORDON: *(Getting upset.)* What are you —

[RUTH: Ivo, if you've something to ask, you should just come out and ask it.]

IVO: Have you heard of Doctor Emma Uda?

GORDON: Hasn't everyone?

IVO: So, you know what she does?

GORDON: Yes.

IVO: Were you going to see Doctor Uda?

GORDON: Our baby was already dead. What would I need to see Doctor Uda for?

IVO: So, no?

GORDON: No.

IVO: Did you speak with the Captain about the weather?

GORDON: Yes, I did.

IVO: What was that conversation?

GORDON: I expressed concern about the weather. I said we were fine either way — that we wouldn't blame him if it was too rough to travel.

IVO: He said you were very insistent on going. He said you offered him money to help him make his decision.

GORDON: There was another couple on the boat. It must have been that man.

IVO: He said it was the man who's wife fell in the water — that you offered him extra money to cross in the bad weather.

GORDON: Well, it wasn't me. I didn't offer him anything.

IVO: Why did you take the clip?

GORDON: Which clip?

IVO: The clip on the ferry? As it pulled away we have a record of you taking a ten second clip of Lily looking out at the water.

GORDON: *(Shaky.)* Oh . . .

IVO: Why did you take that clip? It doesn't seem like this was a point in time you'd want to remember, add to the family reel . . .

GORDON: I . . . I don't know. It was an impulse. I can't explain it. *(With difficulty.)* She just looked really . . . her hair in that light . . . I . . . ?

IVO: *(Seeing Gordon's difficulty.)* Alright. Thank you.

CHERRY DOCS
David Gow

Dramatic
Danny, forties to fifties; Mike, twenties

> *Mike is a skin-head, in prison for committing a vile hate-crime.*
> *Danny is the lawyer appointed to defend him. Danny is Jewish.*

> *Danny and Mike meet, interview room, jail.*

DANNY: How many legal aid lawyers have you met with?

MIKE: What do you mean? *(Pause.)* None.

DANNY: How many before me?

MIKE: In my life?

DANNY: I am going to indulge in a little colloquial language for a moment here. *(Pause.)* Don't get fucking smart with me. *(Mike is taken aback by this.)* That's a little personal commentary, do you understand?

MIKE: Un huh.

DANNY: No?

MIKE: No.

DANNY: No way am I doing this.

> *(Danny begins to close his briefcase.)*

MIKE: What did I do?

DANNY: I don't want to hear 'un huh' from you. The Court is not going to like 'un huh.'

MIKE: What would you like to hear?

DANNY: I'd like to hear you say, "I understand that you were making a little off the record, personal commentary."

MIKE: I understand that you were making a little off the record personal commentary.

DANNY: Mr. Dunkelman.

MIKE: Mr. Dunkelman, sir.

DANNY: Are you being smart?

MIKE: No sir.

(Mike lights a cigarette with a paper match.)

DANNY: Don't call me sir.

MIKE: Right.

DANNY: Do you know what kind of name Dunkelman is?

MIKE: I know it's not Irish.

DANNY: Exactly. It's not Irish, not in the least. It is a Jewish name. Which makes me . . . ?

MIKE: A person with a Jewish name . . . ?

DANNY: Right.

MIKE: You're a Jew?

DANNY: Is that what I said?

MIKE: So you're not?

DANNY: What difference does it make to you?

MIKE: I'd like to know where I stand.

DANNY: If they sent you a legal aid lawyer who's Jewish, how would you feel about that?

MIKE: Works fine for me. Works great when you think about it. Are you any good?

DANNY: No, I failed. I failed everything. My entrance exams, the bars, that's why I'm working as a lawyer. I'm totally incompetent.

MIKE: I like your sense of humour.

DANNY: That's great.

MIKE: Oh. *(Pause.)* Well, I don't mind that you're Jewish if that's what you're wondering about.

DANNY: Thank you, thank you so much. I'll wire my parents. Better, I'll wire Moses. "Moses tell God they're lightening up down here." You are a little prick aren't you?

MIKE: So, your parents are Jewish?

DANNY: Fuck You, sport.

MIKE: You're very angry.

DANNY: I don't like Skinheads, I don't like Neo-Nazis, and I'm not fond of Tattoos. *(Pause.)* I think the crime you're charged with is . . . ugly. *(Pause. Danny closes his briefcase, stands, and is getting ready to leave.)*

So I'm not much inclined to like you. You can ask someone else to be assigned, I think . . .

MIKE: You don't have to like me, I'm not asking anyone to like me.

DANNY: *(Pause.)* That's refreshing.

MIKE: For your knowledge, (for the record), I did the crime. For the record, I was heavily intoxicated.

(The straightforwardness of this makes a minor impression on Danny. A pause.)

DANNY: . . . You say you were intoxicated? Did the police test your blood?

MIKE: No. But I think it was pretty obvious when they picked me up.

DANNY: What did you drink?

MIKE: A fifth of scotch and three or four pints.

DANNY: So you were quite inebriated?

MIKE: I was pissed out of my skull.

DANNY: Anything else?

MIKE: A little pot.

DANNY: Where did the drinking take place?

MIKE: At a concert.

DANNY: Which was . . .

MIKE: By a band called HURC.

DANNY: Is that something to do with Hercules?

MIKE: No.

DANNY: What kind of name is HURC?

MIKE: It stands for Holy Useful Racial Cleansing. *(Short pause.)* It's a pun.

DANNY: *(Nodding.)* Yeah, I got that. *(Looks down and writes for a moment. He then looks at a file.)* It says here you were wearing steel-toed, cherry Doc Martens combat boots, is that right?

MIKE: Yeah, cherry docs. Eighteen holes.

DANNY: It also alleges that you kicked the victim thirty odd times while wearing those boots, is that right?

MIKE: Yes sir.

DANNY: Don't call me sir. *(Pause.)* Why were you wearing those particular boots?

MIKE: Steel toes? It's part of what is a recognizable uniform, Mr. Dunkelman.

DANNY: Do me a favour. Just don't say my name . . . OK?

MIKE: OK.

DANNY: *(Handing Mike a folder.)* Would you mind reading this to me?

MIKE: *(He reads.)* "The victim suffered heavy internal hemorrhaging, and structural damage to the spine, which would have made walking again difficult at best. As well, he had what is referred to as an intellectual impairment, more specifically he was having trouble speaking. The attack is characterized as prolonged, the examining physicians feel it must have lasted two to three minutes." Which is kind of long when you think of it. "He lost sight in one eye as well. He died three weeks after the incident, from related brain trauma."

(A pause. Mike gives the file back to Danny.)

DANNY: Anyway *Mike*, what I'd like to know, to get an idea of how you might present in trial is, how do you feel about this?

MIKE: Can I say something to you?

DANNY: Sure. Are you going to answer my question?

MIKE: Yeah, I will. I just wanted to say you don't look like a Jew.

DANNY: Mnnhmnn. Neither do you. You don't look like . . . a Jew.

(They overlap one another.)

MIKE: I'm not a Jew —

DANNY: You're kidding? Funny, you don't look like a Jew —

MIKE: Knock it off —

DANNY: Are you going to hurt me if I don't — ?

MIKE: Knock it off —

DANNY: OK, Jew boy, anything you say —

MIKE: Would you fucking cut that out — ?

DANNY: *(Loudly.)* So how do you feel about what happened — ?

MIKE: *(Overlapping Danny's last two words.)* Stupid fuckin' Paki. We don't need Paki's on this planet anyway —

(A long pause.)

DANNY: Well that's going to need a little going over. *(Pause.)* I think the gentleman was a South Asian, to begin with. How do you think . . . What kind of defense am I going to concoct for someone like yourself?

MIKE: What do you mean for someone like . . . ?

DANNY: For someone who seems to feel no remorse, who isn't in the least
. . . Who seems fairly happy —

MIKE: I feel remorse. I didn't want to kill him. I wasn't trying to kill him.
I feel very sorry that he died. *(Pause.)* I think what you're asking is
uh "how can anyone let alone I, defend a racist, white supremacist,
Skinhead, punk" is that right?

DANNY: Let's assume for a moment, that you're dead on the money.

MIKE: I don't want to be defended as any one of those things.

DANNY: Oh?

MIKE: Because those are my ideas if you follow me. They are completely
separate from who I am as a person. An individual on trial for an
act, an assault, I don't want the movement marked with my crime.

DANNY: You will be very lucky to be convicted of manslaughter, much
more likely second degree murder, I'd look for mitigating —

MIKE: I want to be on trial for what I did, are you following me on that?

DANNY: No.

MIKE: I don't want to be tried as a Skinhead, because then they are trying
the movement and not me.

DANNY: "The movement"?

MIKE: Yeah. It's a movement. A youth movement.

DANNY: Listen *Mike,* a lot of this bullshit makes me very hot under the
collar, do you understand? I'm not sure that makes me the best person to argue your defense. Maybe there are lawyers in your movement who could put forward your case more sympathetically —

MIKE: I don't think so. All I am asking is that I be tried. Not the ideology
of the Skinhead movement.

DANNY: The crown attorney will prosecute you however he or she can, I
would be in the unenviable position of defending you, if we decide
on that.

MIKE: Well. I think you're all right. I think you're a good guy.

DANNY: I frankly don't think a whole lot of you. I'm inclined to think
you're a shit.

MIKE: That's OK. You're going to help me.

DANNY: Am I?

MIKE: Yes.

DANNY: What makes you so certain?

MIKE: The kind of person you are.

DANNY: Which is?

MIKE: Liberal, a liberal thinker. Checks and Balances and everybody deserves a fair trail bla blah bla bla . . .

DANNY: Is that so?

MIKE: Is it wrong? Is it a wrong way to think?

DANNY: Faced with someone like you . . .

MIKE: What kind of person am I?

DANNY: Obviously intelligent. You're not a big planner, I don't think —

MIKE: I could have planned all this.

DANNY: Between beers? *(Somewhat emphatically.)* I don't think you did. I think you got swept along.

MIKE: OK, that's possible . . .

DANNY: Have you got a little check list, an agenda for today?

MIKE: Yup.

DANNY: So where are we?

MIKE: You tell me Danny Dunkelman, where are we?

DANNY: Where do we stand in all of this?

MIKE: Yeah.

DANNY: We stand in shit.

MIKE: What can we do to get out of that position?

DANNY: *(Somewhere else momentarily.)* . . . Look in every direction first, slowly and without moving . . . *(More present.)* The most important thing is that you not say anything to anyone, do you understand?

MIKE: Because it could come back at us later?

DANNY: Yes. That means anyone is a walking tape recorder, with the exception of me.

MIKE: Can I trust you?

DANNY: You can trust me to perform my duties as your attorney.

MIKE: If I need to talk to someone, can I call you?

DANNY: If you need anything in the way of legal counsel and it can't wait, you can call my office. I'll take you through the Preliminary Hearing; After that we'll see.

MIKE: We'll see?

DANNY: Yeah, one step at a time.

MIKE: *(Slight pause.)* Thanks, that's great.

(Mike offers Danny his hand.)

Why?

DANNY: What?

MIKE: Why are you agreeing to represent me?

DANNY: For the preliminary hearing . . . I don't know. I guess it's a big challenge.

MIKE: I'm a big challenge?

DANNY: It ain't your eye colour, sweetheart. You're an intelligent kid. On some level, I find it a little difficult to believe this is a premeditated act. Maybe a Jury would feel the same way. I'll be in touch, keep your mouth shut and your head down.

MIKE: All right boss. OK.

DANNY: *(About to leave.)* Have you got a reason for wanting me, on this?

MIKE: *(Smiling.)* Like I said, you're a liberal. A humanist, liberal Jew. So — you have to do your very best. In an ideal world I'd see you eliminated. In this world I need you more than anyone.

DANNY: . . . Eliminated?

MIKE: Basically.

DANNY: Is that all?

MIKE: What else is there?

(Danny is silent. Mike is getting wound up.)

MIKE: *(Turning his back on Danny.)* . . . Global Fucking Himey Village . . .

(Danny starts a strange, deep laugh, like the kind of laughter you hear after a car accident.)

MIKE: You laughin' at me?

(Danny continues to laugh.)

MIKE: What are you — laughin? What is . . . ?

(Danny continues.)

MIKE: What's laughing supposed to mean?

(Danny bangs his hand on the table three times still laughing.)

DANNY: *(Through a surfeit of laughter.)* Yer killin' me. *Yer' fuckin' killin' me.*

(Lights snap out on the scene.)

CHICKEN
Mike Batistick

Dramatic
Wendell and Floyd, thirties

> *Wendell is under a lot of financial pressure and has decided to train roosters to fight. Floyd is a wayward friend who is staying with him. Here, Wendell explains his cockfight idea to Floyd.*

> *Setting: A cramped apartment in the Bronx. Early afternoon. At rise: Across much of the down and mid-stage — stacked both ankle and knee-high — are piles of envelopes, piles of papers, and several piles of junk. Wendell, an unhealthy looking man, stares at a rooster, which sits in a cage below him. Floyd, his friend, stands nearby.*

WENDELL: *(To Floyd.)* He's a little sick. So he has to stay downstairs for a little while.

FLOYD: OK.

WENDELL: Yeah. Once he's better, he'll go on the roof. With the other ones. Upstairs.

FLOYD: Other ones?

WENDELL: There are four more of them. On the roof.

FLOYD: Lina is gonna kill you.

WENDELL: The healthy ones are in the homing pigeon cages right now. But he's 'spose to be the best one, why isn't he healthy Floyd?

FLOYD: You need to get this bird out of the apartment.

WENDELL: He might die if he goes outside right now.

FLOYD: He's sitting here being sick in your living room.

WENDELL: So?

FLOYD: What if he gives us what he's got? What if he dies in here?

WENDELL: Why are you saying that?

FLOYD: Look at him. You can't just bring these things into your home. He's so sick, they've got stuff on them.

WENDELL: You don't know that.

FLOYD: Didn't you at least ask why he looks so bad?

WENDELL: I think it happens sometimes.

FLOYD: Yeah. It just happens sometimes when you die. Why didn't you ask me about it before you bought it?

WENDELL: I didn't buy it.

FLOYD: Then where'd you get this thing?

WENDELL: Geronimo.

FLOYD: *(Beat.)* What?

WENDELL: Geronimo.

FLOYD: You're kiddin', right?

WENDELL: Look, I know you're still pissed at him.

FLOYD: Pissed at him?

WENDELL: You gotta get over this, Floyd.

FLOYD: *Pissed at him?* He's the reason I'm in this situation in the first place.

WENDELL: All you had to do was patch up old tires and help him raise chickens in the back.

FLOYD: He should be deported.

WENDELL: Look, I'm sorry he fired you, but welcome to one of his birds. *(Beat.)* Floyd. You know you can stay here as long as you want, but like . . . you can't, either.

FLOYD: My dad would think you're insane bringin' a bird in the house.

WENDELL: Speakin' of your dad —

FLOYD: I was not speakin' of my dad —

WENDELL: I called him up. He gave me a recipe to condition this thing. Like a diet plan. He said you'd know how to put it together right.

FLOYD: You called him up?

WENDELL: Yeah. He sorta ran out of juice towards the end, I didn't get the whole thing, and he's really hard to understand now, but he said you'd know how to administer it. Maybe you can call him up and get the rest of it. It's a morning-of thing, to get the birds excited before the fight.

FLOYD: Wendell?

WENDELL: What?

FLOYD: What are you doing?

WENDELL: *(Hard for him.)* Lina's about to pop with the baby, Floyd. You been loafin' on my couch for like three months. I got no fucking money left, her belly is getting bigger and bigger. You're gonna train this bird and then you're movin' out with the money.

FLOYD: *(Beat.)* Wendell. I got nowhere to go.

WENDELL: I'll help you find somewhere.

FLOYD: Wendell —

WENDELL: Thirty-five thousand if we win. You're the half Cuban, your people's DNA is built for this shit, you're the only person I know who even knows how to *look* at a fighting rooster.

FLOYD: Wendell —

WENDELL: It's in Washington Heights, Geronimo sucks at winning these things, he hasn't won since you left, you gotta do this Floyd. *(Beat.)* Then you gotta move out.

FLOYD: When your baby girl comes you're gonna ask yourself again and again why you didn't reach for that rubber two trimesters ago. A cockfight's not gonna help things.

WENDELL: Yeah it will.

FLOYD: This shit's illegal.

WENDELL: Illegal?

FLOYD: Don't you work for, like, the city?

WENDELL: So?

FLOYD: You should have ethics.

WENDELL: I collect tolls all day on the Whitestone Bridge. Ethics?

FLOYD: I got a strong feeling you're only shooting girl bullets.

WENDELL: Excuse me?

FLOYD: There is no doubt that your child is a girl. Look at the way you're behavin'. Take this piece-of-poultry-shit back to Geronimo and his smelly tire-pile-of-a-tire-shop and just let it go.

WENDELL: Floyd —

FLOYD: Filipino gypsy. He's gettin' in your head.

WENDELL: How?

FLOYD: Like he did. When we were kids.

WENDELL: He just wants you to show up to work on time.

FLOYD: Back of his tire shop hatchin' roosters so he can fight in Washington Heights? Filipinos: They do curses on you. He did his flip gypsy curse all over you and this bird. Putting his sad, third world face on, jealous we speak English *better,* I'm glad I quit his shop —

WENDELL: You got fired —

FLOYD: This bird's a mutt, look at it. It's sick. Any bird that's ever come outta the back a that shop that ever worked *I* built. I did not have a hand in this thing. I do not make sick birds.

WENDELL: Floyd.

FLOYD: What?

WENDELL: Apparently this thing is modified.

FLOYD: *(Beat.)* What?

WENDELL: He's enhanced. He's special.

FLOYD: What are you talkin' about?

WENDELL: Geronimo has added specifications. To his genes.

FLOYD: What? How?

WENDELL: He got a hold of some hormone. He put it in both bird's parents. His four brothers are just like him. Go look on the roof. They're huge. Plus you gotta see his moms.

FLOYD: *(Interested, but trying to hide it.)* She big?

WENDELL: His moms looks like Nell Carter.

FLOYD: What?

WENDELL: Yeah. Like *Gimme a Break.*

FLOYD: Wendell. Having a mom like Nell Carter, Wendell, I don't know if that's . . .

WENDELL: What?

FLOYD: Positive.

WENDELL: Sure it is.

FLOYD: Nell Carter's heart stopped at like forty.

WENDELL: *(Beat.)* Floyd. This thing's a Calagay.

FLOYD: A what?

WENDELL: A Calagay fighting rooster from Calagay, France.

FLOYD: France.

WENDELL: Yeah.

FLOYD: Like, Europe?

WENDELL: Yeah, like France. Calagay, France. *(Floyd examines the rooster more closely, perhaps approaching the cage.)*

FLOYD: France, huh?

WENDELL: Yeah. France.

FLOYD: How'd Nimo get him over here if he's from France?

WENDELL: Things from France are sophisticated.

FLOYD: Listen to you, you already *sound* like him.

WENDELL: Well it's true. France is classy.

FLOYD: You're a native born American and you just sounded like the City of Manila. "France is sophisticated," I can hear him sayin' it.

WENDELL: You walk outside today Floyd? Half of Haiti lives out there now there's so much French.

FLOYD: So?

WENDELL: You want to let these people beat you? This is *your* country.

FLOYD: This country put me in an orphanage.

WENDELL: Poor fucking baby. Me too.

FLOYD: Don't we have enough roosters over here that we don't have to import them from France?

WENDELL: A chicken is a chicken.

FLOYD: *No.* A chicken is a girl chicken. A rooster is a boy chicken. All of them are birds. A chicken is not just a chicken, no wonder Geronimo conned you.

WENDELL: Cut his feathers, Floyd. We're gonna at least make him look good if he's gonna get his ass kicked.

FLOYD: That's the entirely wrong attitude to have, you thinking he's gonna get his ass kicked.

WENDELL: Cut his feathers like a fighting bird then I'll think whatever you want. I'll get you vitamins and supplements, you're gonna cut his feathers, you're gonna train this bird, then you're moving out.

FLOYD: No I'm not.

WENDELL: Yes you are.

FLOYD: I'm staying right here.

WENDELL: Stop pretending like you live here.

FLOYD: I do live here.

WENDELL: No. You. Don't. *(Pause.)*

FLOYD: *(A bit scared.)* You're serious.

WENDELL: Like a big piece of cancer. *(Another pause. Floyd examines the bird some more.)*

FLOYD: I gotta say.

WENDELL: What?

FLOYD: It's a very handsome rooster.

WENDELL: *(Beat.)* It is, isn't it?

FLOYD: Yeah. So he's modified.

WENDELL: Yeah. He's modified. From another continent. *(Beat.)* Floyd, I am so not fucking around with this. *(Beat.)* I'm going to get something to eat. I'm starving.

FLOYD: We just ate.

WENDELL: I'm hungry.

FLOYD: How?

WENDELL: I appreciate it, you cutting his feathers.

FLOYD: No problem.

WENDELL: These things are so depressing until somebody cuts their feathers.

FLOYD: Probably gonna be depressing afterwards too.

WENDELL: No. From here on out we talk positive. I'm goin' to get food. That's positive. Five French birds. That's positive. This chicken —

FLOYD: Rooster —

WENDELL: The rooster. Is positive. The entire planet is going to be a radioactive glow of positivity from here on out, OK?

FLOYD: *(Beat.)* OK.

WENDELL: Thank you for agreeing to cut his feathers.

FLOYD: No problem.

WENDELL: Just make sure you do it on the roof.

THE DIRTY TALK
Michael Puzzo

Comic
Lino and Mitch, thirties to forties

> *Lino and Mitch are stuck in a cabin in the mountains during a grinding rain storm. They met in an internet chat room, where Lino was impersonating a woman.*

> *The door bursts open and in walks a seething, soaking wet Mitch covered in grease and clutching the tattered skeletal remains of an umbrella. He stands momentarily stunned; breathing heavily, he erupts into a violent fit of rage and proceeds to beat the umbrella to death.*

MITCH: You useless, useless . . . Motherless piece a shit . . . Fucking evil . . . *Evil* . . . Totes! *(Exhausted by the tirade, drops the umbrella.)* Goddamn *Water World* outside! *(Shaking the water from his hair, walks over to the bathroom.)* Soaked. *(Ferociously searching the bathroom.)* Where are the fucking towels!!! *(Charges out of the bathroom and points at Lino.)* You!!! *(Lino, a little confused, points at himself, but Mitch makes a beeline back to the umbrella, leaps on it like a lion on a gazelle and begins to stomp it ferociously into the ground.)* Here's your fucking partly cloudy, chance of showers! Why . . . don't you just . . . Fucking . . . *Die!!! (Pause.)*

LINO: I don't think it can hurt you anymore.

MITCH: Hey!

LINO: It's "Lino" actually.

MITCH: Stop. Do not say your name. I don't want that inconsequential information cluttering up my brain. Soon you will no longer be present here. But as long as you are, you have no name, understand?

LINO: Sorry, Mitch.

MITCH: My name is also forbidden. *(Walking around the room examining*

the writing on the boxes, and then realizing something, spins around.)
Wait a second, what do you think you're doing?

LINO: What do you mean?

MITCH: What did I say to you before I went outside to start the car?

LINO: Um, "Drop Dead you little F'ing Freak"?

MITCH: Don't be cute. After that!

LINO: Um . . . I . . . Oh, I know. "Don't make yourself comfortable."

MITCH: And?

LINO: Oh, *(Giggles.)* I would hardly call this comfortable.

MITCH: Up!

LINO: *(Giggles.)* You must need a Dramamine before you go to —

MITCH: Stop. Get up!

LINO: OK, OK. *(Struggles to get up but the motion of the waves make it difficult.)* You may have to throw me a life preserver.

MITCH: *Get the fuck off the bed . . . Now!!!*

LINO: OK, OK —

MITCH: No, no more "bed" talk.

LINO: But —

MITCH: Enough, unless you want me to do an "umbrella" on you.

LINO: Mmmmmm!

MITCH: You sick little freak!

LINO: What?

MITCH: That was a "yummy" sound! No, fucking "yummy" sounds in relation to me!

LINO: I'm sorry, you're right, that was . . . inappropriate. I'll try and follow the rules.

MITCH: Good. Now get outta my sight. *(To himself.)* OK, now where's the hell the phone?

LINO: Um, is it OK if I sit?

MITCH: Do what you want. *(Looking through his wallet.)* OK, Triple A . . . good . . .

LINO: I hate to bother you again, but, um, where?

MITCH: *(Picking up the phone.)* Where what?

LINO: Am I allowed to sit?

MITCH: I don't care, sit . . . *(Dialing.)* . . . sit on one of the boxes. *(Into the phone.)* Hello, Hello!

LINO: *(Looking around at boxes.)* They all say "Glass."

MITCH: So stand! *(Into phone.)* Hello! Wait, they can't all say "Glass"? None of them say "Towels"?

LINO: I don't think so. *(Looks at more boxes.)* Oh, wait, this one says "Gardening Tools and Christmas Decorations."

MITCH: Fucking Bitch! *(Overlapping.)*

LINO: If you want to dry off . . . you could —

MITCH: Some of those towels had to be mine!

LINO: — always use one of the sheets from the —

MITCH: Careful, I *will* take this phone and propel it at you. *(Into the phone.)* Hello, hello? *Hello! (Slams down the receiver. Thunder.)* This is like a B horror movie.

LINO: The phone's dead?

MITCH: You seem to have a talent for stating the obvious.

LINO: I just —

MITCH: Enough —

LINO: I, um . . . OK. *(A tremendous clap of thunder is heard, an awkward pause.)* So, is it supposed to rain like this all day?

MITCH: What do I look like? . . . *The fucking Weather Channel?*

LINO: Look, it's a . . . It's a valid question . . . It's pouring out there and I know —

MITCH: I hate the rain . . . in fact I hate *all* weather . . . Rain, snow, fucking . . . tsunamis!

LINO: You get many tsunamis in Jersey?

MITCH: You know what I mean.

LINO: Actually, I don't really. You hate the weather? What does that mean exactly? It's like saying you hate . . . uuuuh . . . sidewalks. That kinda stuff just happens.

MITCH: Sidewalks do not just happen!

LINO: I know, what I meant is — *(Overlapping.)*

MITCH: Sidewalks are not a natural phenomenon.

LINO: OK.

MITCH: When was the last time you heard . . . "Looks like there's a sixty percent chance of a sidewalk storm —"

LINO: I get your point.

MITCH: — so better stay indoors folks —

LINO: — I was just —

MITCH: "— now back to you Chuck."

LINO: I was just making an analogy.

MITCH: Oh, really. Well, it wasn't a very good one.

LINO: OK . . . Yes, I know, but . . . it's just that the rain —

MITCH: Will you just shut the fuck up about the weather, OK?!?! "Is it supposed to rain like this all day?" Yeah, it's gonna rain "cats and sidewalks," so you better wear a fucking helmet!

LINO: OK, OK, I admit it: Sidewalks was a poor choice of words. I'll think of something —

MITCH: If you wanna think of something, think of a way for us to get the hell outta here.

LINO: Hence, my question about the rain.

MITCH: Yeah . . . you're right . . . I'm gonna go turn on *The Weather Channel. (Goes over to TV and switches it on, but nothing but snow appears.)* C'mon you goddamn ancient Fred Flintstone TV *(Slams on the top of the TV.)* Ahhhhhhh . . . Snow!

LINO: More weather!

MITCH: I really don't like you.

LINO: Yeah, well . . . I don't need the weather report to tell me that.

MITCH: OK, you know what . . . please stop trying to be clever. You're really bad at it. In fact, just stop talking all together.

LINO: Sorry. I'm just trying to make the best of a bad situation.

MITCH: Yeah, great . . . but you're making it —

LINO: Worse?

MITCH: Yeah, much worse.

LINO: Sorry, I tend to do that. *(Pause, changing the subject.)* Um, so, no luck with the car, huh?

MITCH: Flooded.

LINO: Wow. It's actually flooded? What, did you leave the windows rolled down?

MITCH: What is that, another joke?

LINO: No.

MITCH: It's flooded, it's fucking flooded. The . . . the . . . the engine is flooded or the starter or the . . . I don't fucking know. Look, *car no go!*

LINO: I don't drive.

MITCH: Besides . . . I don't . . . I don't have any windshield wipers.

LINO: You mean they don't work?

MITCH: No, I don't have any. I had them, but I . . . I got into an argument with . . . Look, I ripped them off, OK?

LINO: Why?

MITCH: Hey, Regis, enough with the fucking questions, OK? All you need to know is we can't drive down the mountain.

LINO: Until the rain stops.

MITCH: Yeah, until the rain stops. Goddammit, I thought he said he had a satellite dish or some shit . . . Well, *The Weather Channel* wouldn't be any help anyway. You turn that shit on cuz you wanna go to the beach or something and it's always like, the weather for Yuma, Arizona, or fucking Tupelo, Mississippi! I mean, who the hell needs to know the weather in Tupelo?

LINO: Well —

MITCH: And if you dare say, "People who live in Tupelo," I swear to Christ I'll tie a pork chop around your neck and let the bears eat you.

LINO: I wasn't going to, uh . . . Bears?

MITCH: Yeah . . . *big ones.*

LINO: I wasn't going to say that.

MITCH: Bullshit.

LINO: I wasn't. I was going to say . . .

MITCH: Bullshit. I've known you for what? Like twenty minutes and already I can write your dialogue for you. Like you were the cutesy, annoying neighbor on fucking . . . "Must See TV"!

LINO: You think I'm cute?

MITCH: Christ, maybe I should just tie the pork chop around my own neck. *(Pause.)*

LINO: People who travel.

MITCH: Excuse me?

LINO: People who travel . . . to Mississippi . . . for like, vacation.

MITCH: Well, of course. Mississippi's booming travel industry!

LINO: Well, actually —

MITCH: "Where should we go this year baby? Club Med or Mississippi?"

LINO: My sister and her husband went to —

MITCH: I bet it's a real hot spot for like . . . sentimental Klan members —

LINO: Mississippi now has a —

MITCH: Meet Harriet Tubman . . . Go for a ride on the Underground
Railroad —

LINO: They have like, a riverboat casino —

MITCH: Kids, sure can't get enough of those chain gangs —

LINO: OK! *(Pause.)* You are just plain . . . Mean, you know that?

MITCH: Mean? I'm "mean." Jesus, what are you, fucking ten? I'm just a
big ol' Meany.

LINO: Yes . . . and it doesn't suit you.

MITCH: It doesn't suit me?

LINO: Yes, and could you please stop doing that? Repeating everything I
say. It's like you're just riffing until you can think of some new, sarcastic, hateful . . . "Mean" thing to say.

MITCH: What do you want me to do, say *"I'm sorry"*? OK, fine, I'm sorry.

LINO: Please don't patronize me. You're not sorry! You said it yourself you
don't like me!!! Well, um, I have news for you too . . . Buddy. You
are not exactly the man I thought you were going to be, either!

MITCH: *(Taken aback.)* Yeah . . . well . . . I've heard that before. *(Pause.)*
It's just that . . . you lied to me. You fucking lied to me. And now
this . . . this whole situation is . . . Look, I'm just feeling a little —

LINO: Embarrassed? Humiliated?

MITCH: What? No!

LINO: Emasculated?

MITCH: *No!* What I am is . . . *wet!!!* Look at me! I am *soaking fucking wet!!!*
(Wringing out his wet shirt.) And look at this, *(Points to a grease
stain.)* this is my favorite shirt! *(Gets up and starts checking the label-
ing on the boxes.)* Shit, I can't believe she took all the towels and left
me with the fucking gardening tools! *(Kicks one of the boxes labeled
"Glass" across the room.)* What am I doing? What the fuck am I
doing? *(Breaks down.)* She didn't even leave me a dishtowel! Not
even a washrag . . . *(Pause.)*

LINO: It's OK. *(Lino moves tentatively toward Mitch to comfort him.)*

MITCH: Get the fuck away from me!

LINO: I just. . .

MITCH: Get away . . . Go stand over there. Go! Move! Now! The other
side of the cabin!

LINO: Couldn't we —

MITCH: *Now! (Pause.)*

LINO: OK.

MITCH: Get behind the dresser.

LINO: Are you kidding?

MITCH: No. Pull it out and get behind it.

LINO: It looks heavy.

MITCH: Good. *(Lino goes to the dresser and struggles to pull it out.)*

LINO: Can you give me a hand?

MITCH: No.

LINO: No?

MITCH: Absolutely not.

LINO: OK. . . . Can I just ask you something?

MITCH: Are you behind the dresser?

LINO: Um, well, not yet.

MITCH: You can ask me something, when you're behind the dresser.

LINO: Oh, OK.

MITCH: All the way behind!

LINO: I don't have a lot of upper body strength.

MITCH: Too bad.

LINO: I'm not really good at athletics.

MITCH: I'm sorry?

LINO: Sports. I'm not good at sports.

MITCH: Dude, moving a dresser is not an Olympic event.

LINO: You're starting again.

MITCH: What?

LINO: Starting with me! Like with the sidewalk thing. Like you're gonna say . . . *(Labors with the dresser.)* Shoot, this is heavy. What do you have in here anyway?

MITCH: The body of the last motherfucker who asked me too many questions.

LINO: I thought you said you never did this before.

ELECTION DAY

Josh Tobiessen

Comic

Clark, twenties to thirties; Adam, twenties

Today is the day of a local election and Clark is running for Mayor. He's going door-to-door and asking for votes. Adam's girlfriend Brenda is out campaigning for Clark's opponent. Here, Clark makes his pitch to Adam, who basically doesn't care at all about the election, much to Brenda's annoyance.

Brenda's apartment. There is a sustained knocking at the front door, which brings Adam out of the bedroom to answer it. He opens the door to find a man in a sharp looking suit. As soon as he opens the door he remembers Cleo's bag of bombs on the counter.

CLARK: You're not Brenda.

ADAM: No, she's not here. Are you —

CLARK: No, the mailbox downstairs says Brenda Zerkowski on it.

ADAM: I'm Adam, her partner, boyfriend, whatever.

CLARK: Boyfriend, say boyfriend. Partner could mean anything.

ADAM: You want to leave a message or something? She should be back for lunch soon.

CLARK: Yeah, I got a message, but it's a message for everyone. I'm going door to door today, around your neighborhood, trying to get people to come out and vote.

ADAM: Yeah, thanks, I'm not interested.

CLARK: In voting?

ADAM: No, I'm definitely voting. But you're trying to tell me who to vote for, right?

CLARK: I can't *tell* you to do anything Adam. Can I?

ADAM: Well, right.

CLARK: So what are you worried about?

ADAM: I just have a lot to do. I'm busy.

CLARK: I respect that, it's good to keep busy. And because I see you're a busy man, I'm going to keep this brief.

ADAM: I'm really busy.

CLARK: I'll be quick.

(Clark moves past Adam into the apartment. As he begins his speech he takes out a hand held tape player that plays patriotic music and gives it to Adam to hold.)

CLARK: Our city is facing a plague my friend, a plague of fiscal irresponsibility and corruption at all levels of leadership. Our children's futures are compromised, our public safety is ignored, and all the while taxes continue to rise like a rocket, hurting our local industries and kicking hard working citizens like you and me right in the wallet.

It's time to bring respectability back to our local government. It's time to bring smiles to the faces of our innocent little children. It's time for Americans everywhere to be proud to see their flag waving high over our city hall. I'm the man that's going to make that happen this time, and I hope that you'll vote for me.

ADAM: You?

CLARK: Yeah. Jerry Clark.

ADAM: You're Jerry Clark?

CLARK: Yeah.

ADAM: I thought you were older.

(Jerry takes back his tape player and stops the music.)

CLARK: That was my dad.

ADAM: That makes sense.

CLARK: But you're right. I'm young, like you. Not your typical politician. So do I have your vote?

ADAM: Well, probably not . . . I'm not actually supposed to vote for you.

CLARK: You're not supposed to?

ADAM: I mean, I don't think I'm going to.

CLARK: You don't think so?

ADAM: No. I'm sorry. But thanks for stopping by.

CLARK: Wow, that's . . . OK. I mean, that's your choice of course. That's the beauty of this wonderful country in which we live. Freedom to make bad decisions.

ADAM: I'm sorry.

CLARK: Yeah. You and me both. Wow. Hey listen: you think I could get a glass of water? Just all this walking I've been doing today, probably should have brought a bottle.

ADAM: Ah . . .

CLARK: Come on, it'll only be a minute. You think I don't have other places to be today?

ADAM: Sure sorry, come on in.

(Clark picks up a photograph from a shelf.)

CLARK: This is you and Brenda here?

ADAM: Yeah.

CLARK: She is cute. Are you guys serious?

ADAM: Well, I'm moving in today. So, yeah, pretty serious.

(Adam goes to the kitchen to get Clark a glass of water.)

CLARK: Actually, you got anything besides water?

ADAM: *(Looking in fridge.)* Let's see. We have some juice?

CLARK: You know what? Give me one of those beers in there. It's been a hard morning. You're not going to vote for me, you can at least give me a beer.

ADAM: I guess that's fair.

CLARK: This is the only kind you got?

ADAM: Yeah.

CLARK: Have one with me. Be social.

(Clark comes in and sits on couch. Adam gets a beer but stays standing.)

CLARK: So, Adam. You always vote how Brenda tells you?

ADAM: What?

CLARK: Well, she's the reason isn't she? The reason you're 'not supposed' to vote for me?

ADAM: No, that's not it.

CLARK: No?

ADAM: No.

CLARK: Good. Because, vote for me, don't vote for me: that's one thing, I respect that, but doing something just because your girlfriend wants you to?

ADAM: It's not like that.

CLARK: Good. Thanks for the beer by the way.

ADAM: Sure.

CLARK: So, if it's not her then why aren't you voting for me? If I can ask.

ADAM: No, of course, that's fair enough. I . . . just think your views on certain social issues are . . . wrong.

CLARK: Like what?

ADAM: Like your policies.

CLARK: Which ones?

ADAM: Well, like I don't think your environmental policies are very good.

CLARK: How?

ADAM: Not good for the environment.

CLARK: In what way are they not good for the environment?

ADAM: Lots of ways.

CLARK: So tell me. I want to know. I want to know what I'm doing wrong. *(Beat.)* You say you're going to vote for the other guy, I kind of take it as an insult if you can't give me a good reason. I mean that makes sense to you doesn't it?

ADAM: It's not meant as an insult. At all.

CLARK: But you see what I'm saying though. The point I'm making. You don't like me but you can't give me any reasons why you don't like me. Does that sound fair?

ADAM: It's not about liking you. I'm sure you're a very nice person.

CLARK: I am.

ADAM: It's just a question of your politics.

CLARK: You don't seem to know my politics.

ADAM: Not off the top of my head.

CLARK: Should we wait for Brenda to get back? I'm kidding. You know what? That's fine. You don't actually know who to vote for. That's what we've established here. Right? You're an undecided voter.

ADAM: I'm not undecided.

CLARK: Adam, Adam. Listen to me. You're not an idiot, right?

ADAM: What?

CLARK: I think that I'm right in assuming that you are not an idiot. You agree?

ADAM: Yeah.

CLARK: Politics just isn't your thing. Which is fine, which is absolutely fine. I'm sure that there are things that you care very much about, things that you're very knowledgeable about. What do you do?

ADAM: I'm a graphic designer.

CLARK: Oh, yeah? Like posters?

ADAM: Posters, advertisements mainly.

CLARK: OK. There you go. That's your thing, your specialty. Graphic design. I need some posters, I'll come to you. You have a card?

ADAM: Yeah, um, here.

(Adam gives Clark a card.)

CLARK: See, I'm taking your card. You just got some business. I need an ad designed, some posters, I go to you. Right? Good. Now, I need a steak.

ADAM: A steak?

CLARK: Yeah, a big juicy steak. I got this girl coming over for dinner, a *theoretical* girl of course because in real life I'm happily married, but suppose I want to make this girl some steaks. They've got to be the best I can get because I'm looking to impress. Do I come to you?

ADAM: No?

CLARK: No, of course not. That's not your thing. Posters is your thing, I go to a butcher. That's his thing. And I don't go to a butcher I haven't met before. I go to a butcher that I know, that I have a relationship with. I'd better be looking good for this date too right? This hypothetical date. I need a haircut. Do I come to you?

ADAM: No.

CLARK: Of course not. Where do I go?

ADAM: Barber.

CLARK: Exactly. That's his thing. A barber that I know, one that I've met before. Now you're getting the picture. So now. You need someone to run your city. Do you go to the butcher or the barber?

ADAM AND CLARK: No!

CLARK: The graphic designer?

ADAM AND CLARK: No!

CLARK: All smart people but running a city is not their area of expertise. It is, however, my area of expertise. I'm a politician. And *now* I'm a politician you *know*. You know the other guy?

ADAM: No.

CLARK: He's an asshole. And that's fine if you don't believe me, but do you really want to vote for a guy that you don't even know?

ADAM: I guess that's a good point.

CLARK: It is a good point.

ADAM: Yeah.

CLARK: So . . .

ADAM: You've made some good points, and I think you've convinced me to read some more about the issues before I decide who—

CLARK: I'm telling you who. Me.

ADAM: OK, that's your —

CLARK: You don't trust me? You think I'm not a trustworthy person? I'm telling you who the best man for the job is. It's not a hard decision, alright? Vote for me. Vote Clark.

ADAM: *(Beat.)* Alright, fine. I will . . . Thanks for stopping by.

CLARK: You trying to get rid of me?

ADAM: No, I just know you have other people to see today.

CLARK: You're not going to vote for me are you?

ADAM: I will.

CLARK: You are fucking lying to me.

ADAM: I'm not.

CLARK: I can't believe this. Because of your girlfriend. You told me you were your own man. Did we not establish that earlier?

ADAM: I am.

CLARK: I don't know Adam. It sounds to me like you're not. Like you were lying to me. And you know, I can take it that not everyone is going to vote for me. I disagree with them, but they have their reasons and I can respect that. But this. This is just wrong, and what kills me is that you know it's wrong. You make me want to take a shit. Where's your bathroom.

ADAM: Through there.

CLARK: You're being weak Adam. This city needs people who are strong. Think about that while I'm in there.

EXTREMELY
Rolin Jones

Comic
Johnny and Josh, late teens to early twenties

Johnny and Josh are "extreme sports" fanatics.

Johnny (suited up for wintry fearlessness) stands at the top of a mountain, an extreme snowboard under his feet, that look in his eyes, please. You never had that look. You don't even know what that look is about.

JOHNNY: Broke my collarbone riding a mountain bike in Death Valley. Dislocated my shoulder on a category six rapid. Went cliff diving in Costa Rica, punctured a lung, shattered eight ribs. Had a finger sewn back on. Even tried something called lava hockey. Yeah. Pretty fucked up. But that's how I live. I'm an extreme sportsman.
(Johnny's best friend, Josh, walks up with an extreme snowboard tucked under one arm, squeezing an extreme hand grip, working his extreme forearm.)

JOHNNY: *(Continued.)* I don't belong to a gym. I don't play beer league softball with the guys at work. I don't have a fantasy football team. I live. Extremely.

JOSH: Who are you talking to, Johnny?

JOHNNY: Them.

JOSH: Tsup.

JOHNNY: This is Josh. Tell them why we board.
(Johnny reaches into his snowsuit, grabs an extreme drink. Pop. Chug. Crush. Hyped.)

JOSH: We fucking board because we're fucking bored. Tsup. No, I don't know man, I got into extreme boarding because I was tired of the fucking system, you know what I mean? Nine reasons to blow your fucking head off five times a day, seven days a week, get old, shit in a bag, look over at your old lady, she's growing a mustache. Fuck that.

(Josh hands Johnny the forearm grip. Josh pulls out a beer. Chug. Guzzle. Crush. Buzzed.)

JOHNNY: *(Working the forearm.)* I met Josh at AA. Bunch of sob stories with that crew. Hi, my name is Dickhead and I'm weak. Hi, Dickhead, I've been sober for three days. Way to go, Dickhead. Group therapy, pity party, circle jerk, call it what you want. I needed something else. So I locked eyes with Josh here and we dedicated our lives to living on the edge.

JOSH: I love beer.

JOHNNY: Josh still drinks.

JOSH: I fucking love beer.

JOHNNY: I do too, but not before I board. You end up pissing in your snowsuit and the ladies aren't fucking feeling that back at the lodge.

(Josh locks into his snowboard.)

JOSH: Beer don't break your heart.

JOHNNY: See y'all down at the bottom.

JOSH: Suck it. . . .

JOSH: Tsup.

JOSH AND JOHNNY: . . . Exxttrreeemmmeeee!

JOHNNY: . . . It's kinda extreme. Mildly extreme. And I could do that mountain all day if I wanted to but Josh here is on parole. And they got all these goddamn rules about firearms. And well, we stole these snowboards. We work at the Simi Valley Sizzler. Not that bullshit Sizzler off the one eighteen. Those dudes suck. We're at the one near the Reagan Library.

(Johnny rips off his snow gear. He's wearing his preppy best. Josh finishes the beer and belches.)

JOSH: Protein.

JOHNNY: What's wrong with a power bar?

JOSH: I don't know, what's wrong with being gay?

(Josh hits him in the nut sack. Johnny falls to his knees. Josh rips off his snow clothes. Underneath he's wearing chinos and a gold shirt.)

JOSH: What Johnny's taking forever to say is you don't need a board and a fucking mountain to be extreme. Extreme's a state of mind, man.

It's a guide for living. It's like the other day. We get invited to a work party. We work at the Sizzler over by the Reagan Library.

JOHNNY: I told them that already.

JOSH: Dude, that bitch had Alzheimer's. You think that's easy?

JOHNNY: No one cares.

JOSH: You think it's easy waking up one morning you're the President of the United States, the next you're taking a shit, pointing at the bowl, saying look I made apple pie. Tsup.

JOHNNY: So corporate throws this party for both the Sizzler's in the Simi Valley area.

JOHNNY: *(Holes up two shuttlecocks.)* Two cocks.

JOSH: Four if you're counting ourselves.

JOHNNY: Good one.

JOSH: Tsup.

JOHNNY: And that's cool for about thirty seconds but it gets fucking boring again. So we get another racket, throw in another cock.
(They each pick up another racket. Extreme shuttlecock ballet.)

JOHNNY: That's four rackets, three cocks.

JOSH: Five if you're counting ourselves.

JOHNNY: Funny the first time.

JOSH: Bor-ing.

JOHNNY: And he's right. It ain't extreme.

JOSH: So, we each take a handful of icy hot and wipe it on our balls.

JOSH AND JOHNNY: . . . *(As they rub.)* Exxxttttrrreeemmmeeee.
(They pick up their rackets.)
. . . *(Extreme badminton with extreme pain in the groin region. The game builds quickly. Johnny and Josh are nearly brought to their knees before Johnny summons the uber extreme within him. Takes out his gun and shoots Josh in the leg. Josh falls to the ground and Johnny slams all four shuttlecocks into Josh's face. . .)*

JOHNNY: Beg for the ice. Beg for the ice.

JOSH: *Come on! Come on!*

JOHNNY: Beg for it!

JOSH: *Please! Please!*
(Josh opens the ice chest. They both plunge ice into their pants.)

JOSH: You fucking shot me, man.

(There's a beat. A friendship hangs in the balance.)

JOSH: Extreme.

JOHNNY: Extreme.

JOHNNY AND JOSH: Eexxttrreeemmmeee.

JOHNNY: . . . Gonna own my own business one day.

JOSH: We got fired from Sizzler.

JOHNNY: I'm taking night classes in accounting over at Cal State Northridge.

JOSH: Cal State Nowhere.

JOHNNY: Beats Cal State Radio Shack.

JOSH: Fuck you.

JOHNNY: And Cal State Outback Steakhouse.

JOSH: Yeah, you're the smart guy.

JOHNNY: Or Cal State Glory Hole.

JOSH: Let's move on.

JOHNNY: That girl was a dude.

JOSH: I had like eight long island ice teas, man.

JOHNNY: . . . We don't use parachutes.

JOSH: Yeah, fuck parachutes.

JOHNNY: Parachutes are for John Q Public and his back-up band, the Pussies.

JOHNNY: . . . We're extreme. You don't know what we know. Josh and I? We're the beard hiding the weak chin of America. So in twenty years when China takes to the Pacific and does its best Kimbo Slice on your corn-syrup bodies, don't come crying to us.

JOSH: *(Pissed.)* And if you see our old shift manager, tell him I'm real sorry I forgot to re-up the taco bar.

JOHNNY: And when you tell him that have him crane his fat fucking neck up to the sky, cause we're about to fucking bomb his ass.

JOSH: It's cold up here man. Rarified air.

JOHNNY: Don't tell me, man. Tell them.

JOSH: Tsup.

JOHNNY AND JOSH: Eexxttrreemmmeee!

(They dive extremely.)

THE FARNSWORTH INVENTION

Aaron Sorkin

Dramatic
Sarnoff, forties to fifties; Philo, thirties

> *David Sarnoff is determined to win the race to patent a new tech-*
> *nology which will enable both sound and pictures to be broadcast*
> *— what will soon be known as "television." He has bet on an*
> *inventor named Zworykin, but it looks like an independent genius*
> *named Philo T. Farnsworth is going to beat him to the finish line.*
> *Here, Sarnoff and Farnsworth meet for the first time.*

> *Philo has turned around and sees Sarnoff on the other side of*
> *the stage.*

SARNOFF: I'm David Sarnoff.

PHILO: Philo Farnsworth.

SARNOFF: Sure.

PHILO: You came all the way down from New York?

SARNOFF: Yeah.
  (Beat.)
  What did you say to Zworykin?

PHILO: Hm?

SARNOFF: For posterity's sake. Did you tell him to fuck off?

PHILO: No. I asked him how he fell on the mosaic pattern for light
  storage.

SARNOFF: How did he do it?

PHILO: A lab assistant left a tube in an oven too long. The silver boiled up
  into little pieces. You should find out the name of that lab assistant
  and write it down somewhere. He and Cliff Gardner built the first
  television.

SARNOFF: Listen, I'm sure your lawyer's told you that this decision has no legal effect on your patent, just ours.

PHILO: Is that right?

SARNOFF: No I mean it.

PHILO: You ever hear of Elisha Gray?

SARNOFF: No.

PHILO: He invented the telephone. Then showed up at the patent office exactly 120 minutes after Alexander Graham Bell.

SARNOFF: This isn't like that. You're free to license your patent and so are we.

PHILO: And in a side by side comparison between RCA and The Farnsworth Television Company, where do you suppose the manufacturers are gonna go? I just lost other people's money, I just lost television and I won't lie to you, David, the billion dollars I'm not gonna get might have come in handy, so don't patronize me.

SARNOFF: How did your son die?

PHILO: What?

SARNOFF: I'm sorry, how did your son die?

PHILO: He died of strep throat.

SARNOFF: What are you gonna do now?

PHILO: I have to call my wife and apologize for wasting her time.

SARNOFF: Come work for RCA. We have a lab in Camden, a lab in Schenectady. You move your family there, you're put on salary.

PHILO: I appreciate it but no thank you.

SARNOFF: Why?

PHILO: I don't want to be told what to invent and once I invent it I don't want someone else owning it.

SARNOFF: So what are you gonna do?

PHILO: Well people are starting to talk about fusion.

SARNOFF: I'm sorry?

PHILO: Fusion.

SARNOFF: What is it?

PHILO: It's what powers the rest of the universe. The sun gets its energy from hydrogen particles crashing into each other at hallacious speeds. If we can re-create that in a controlled environment then theoretically all the energy you need to power the world could be found in this pen.

SARNOFF: Where are you gonna get the hydrogen?

PHILO: The whole place is made out of hydrogen.

SARNOFF: You're saying we're not gonna use petroleum?

PHILO: A gallon of water has 100 times the energy as a gallon of gasoline. It doesn't cost anything and you're never gonna run out.

SARNOFF: You're crazy.

PHILO: I heard that a lot when I suggested we could transmit pictures electronically, which was 1922 by the way and there was no reason for your people to humiliate Justin Tolman like that.

SARNOFF: He was an old man with a crumpled piece of paper who'd forgotten a lot of things, including his home address. You sued *me.*

PHILO: Why did Armstrong kill himself?

SARNOFF: Don't believe everything you hear.

PHILO: The guy comes up with frequency modulation, then jumps off the top of a radio tower.

SARNOFF: The same thing killed Armstrong as killed you.

PHILO: You?

SARNOFF: No, but that was a good guess. Alcoholism

PHILO: Maybe.

SARNOFF: Maybe?

PHILO: I know for sure that vomiting-on-my-shoes drunk I'm a better engineer than anyone you've got sober.

SARNOFF: Like I don't know that. Listen, lemme save you some money in psychiatrist bills. You're not pissed off at me, you're pissed off 'cause no one in your lab left a tube in the oven too long. You never got it right.

PHILO: It was a hard problem.

SARNOFF: How hard?

PHILO: I may not have gotten it right, but Zworykin never got it at all and if it weren't for me he'd still be spinning a pin wheel right now.

SARNOFF: Zworykin's a hack, he's second string, he's your understudy. You gave it away.

PHILO: Because he didn't fulfill his potential?

SARNOFF: I meant in relation to —

PHILO: *(Imitating Sarnoff.)* "... the opportunity to lift ourselves intellectually, culturally, spiritually and economically."

SARNOFF: You're a fan?

PHILO: *(Imitating.)* "Radio should be run like a public library. Like a *library,* I say!" What happened to no paid advertising during informational programming?

SARNOFF: I didn't have a choice.

PHILO: You're the president of RCA and the founder of the National Broadcasting Company, you had a variety of choices.

SARNOFF: No I didn't.

PHILO: You know what, David, I think we both blew it huge, but the difference is, I didn't *know* the answer to my light dissipation problem. You *knew* that once there was a financial incentive for an informational broadcast to be popular it would be making a mockery out of both of our lives, to say nothing of a society being informed enough to participate in its own democracy.

SARNOFF: I made one miscalculation in my life and that was that I had no idea how successful it was gonna be at delivering consumers to advertisers. And my friend, once you're good at that you're gonna have a hard time being good at anything else.

PHILO: How hard?

(Silence.)

You said "fuck you" to a Russian soldier when you were 10 but you couldn't say no to advertising dollars? You tried hard but you couldn't?

SARNOFF: God, Phil, that wouldn't have been your way of calling me a kike by any chance, would it?

PHILO: David, I don't give a shit if you think Jesus Christ is the Messiah or not. I'm married to a woman who'll believe in Santa Claus before she'll believe in evolution.

SARNOFF: If you had it to do over, aren't there things you'd do different?

PHILO: If I had it to do over I'd discover an antibiotic for strep throat.

SARNOFF: *(Pause.)* Come work for RCA.

PHILO: Did you come down here to offer me a job?

SARNOFF: No.

(Beat.)

I came down here to tell you that I think your invention is extraordinary.

I wanted to tell you that and to say that it's my intention to be a worthy custodian.

PHILO: *(Pause.)* Good luck.

(Philo extends his hand. Sarnoff shakes it.)

GOD'S EAR

Jenny Schwartz

Comic
Ted and Guy, thirties to forties

> *Ted and Guy have met in a bar and are talking about their wives.*

> *A bar. Ted is drinking beer and watching the game. So is some guy named Guy.*

GUY: Is your wife a wife-wife?

Or is she one a those take-charge, split-your-lip, bust-your-balls, pull-your-chain, cook-your-goose, get-your-goat, rip-you-to-shreds, kick-you-when-you're-down . . . types a gals?

TED: Something like that.

GUY: Best a both, huh?

Lucky guy.

Lucky guy.

Lucky guy.

TED: You want her?

Take her.

She's yours.

GUY: Free a charge?

TED: Small fee.

GUY: Thanks.

Thanks, Man.

Generous offer.

You got yourself a generous spirit.

And that's a rare thing to come by in this day and age.

Trust me on that.

Take it from me.

Trust me on that.

Take it from me.

But I got my own little lady back home to contend with, if you know what I mean.

You know what I mean.

How much we talkin'?

TED: Zero down.

GUY: Money back guarantee?

TED: No questions asked.

GUY: You got a recent photo or what?

(Ted hands Guy a photo.)

TED: Her name's Mel.

Short for Melanoma.

But you can change it.

GUY: Say, not bad.

Those your kids?

TED: Those?

No.

No.

Those are . . .

No.

I should warn you, though, because you can't really tell in the picture:

Her vagina is green and her urine is blue.

GUY: Green, huh?

What, you mean, like, fertile ground?

Or, like, green with envy?

Or, like, cold . . . hard . . . cash?

TED: Something like that.

GUY: And is it a green-green or, like, more like a pastel?

TED: Actually, it's—

Well, I don't want to say lime, but —

GUY: And is this a permanent situation or —

TED: Let me put it this way:

If she's wearing, say, a green camisole or a green bustier or a green negligée or what-have-you, it might bring out the green in her vagina.

Or it might not.

Vaginas are . . .

What's the word?

GUY: Mercurial.

TED: Mercurial.

But it's really only a slight hue.

I just thought I should mention it because of . . .

GUY: Company policy.

TED: Company policy.

So what do you think?

Take her out for a test drive?

Little spin around the block?

One time offer.

Won't last.

Vaginas sell themselves.

GUY: Does she need a lot of light?

TED: A little.

GUY: Water?

TED: The usual.

GUY: Wish I could.

Wish I could.

Wish I could.

But like I said, I got my own little lady back home to contend with, if you know what I mean.

You know what I mean.

How 'bout we do a trade?

My little lady for your little lady?

TED: For keeps?

GUY: Trial basis.

And if we're not completely satisfied, then no big deal, no harm done, no big whoop, no sweat.

I think I got a recent photo here someplace.

(Guy hands Ted a photo.)

GUY: *(Continued.)* Her name's Meg.

Short for Smegma.

But you can change it.

TED: That your daughter?

GUY: Sure is.

TED: That your son?

GUY: Sure was.

TED: Huh . . .

I thought you said your little lady was a little lady.

GUY: Did I?

No kidding.

TED: Don't kid a kidder.

GUY: Did I?

No shit.

TED: Don't shit a shitter.

GUY: Now, don't get me wrong.

I love her to death and all.

But between you, me, and the lamp-post, my little lady is not the little lady I married.

How 'bout Melanoma?

TED: Can I have my recent photo back?

GUY: Is she the little lady you married?

TED: Gimme my recent photo back.

GUY: Gimme gimme never gets.

Cry-baby.

TED: Who you calling cry-baby?

GUY: Wuss.

TED: Who you calling wimp?

GUY: Creep.

TED: Who you calling loser?

GUY: Moron.

TED: Who you calling reject?

GUY: Lame-brain.

TED: Who you calling jerk-off?

GUY: Jack-ass.

TED: Who you calling candy-ass?

GUY: Limp-dick.

TED: Who you calling pecker-head?

GUY: Pansy.

TED: *Gimme my freakin' photo!*

GUY: *Take your freakin' photo!*

TED: *Your wife doesn't know dick about dick!*

(Guy gives Ted back his photo.)

TED: *(Continued.)* What's your favorite part of your job?

GUY: I'm a people person.

TED: I like numbers.

GUY: It's not that I *don't* like numbers . . .

TED: *(Telling a joke.)* What's the difference between your wife and your job?

GUY: What?

TED: After twenty years, your job still sucks.

GUY: Beauty is in the eye of the beer holder.

TED: Good one.

GUY: Beauty is in the eye of the beer holder.

TED: Good one.

GUY: Beauty is in the eye of the beer holder.

TED: Good one.

> *(They are laughing.)*

GUY: I feel for you.

> Is all I'm saying.

> I feel for you.

TED: I don't know you from a hole in the wall.

GUY: I don't know you from Adam.

TED: I don't know you from Adam's house-cat.

GUY: Beat it.

TED: Can it.

GUY: Shove it.

TED: Save it.

GUY: *(Giving him the finger.)* Save this!

> I don't know you from a hole in the ground.

> But I feel for you.

> Man.

TED: Hey Man, don't call me "man".

GUY: Sorry, Man.

TED: *(Giving him the finger.)* Feel this!

LINCOLNESQUE
John Strand

Comic
Francis and Daly, forties

> *Francis, formerly a brilliant political strategist, has a breakdown
> because of his disillusionment with politics and now works as a
> janitor. He also thinks he's Abraham Lincoln. Daly is a political
> kingmaker and an amoral pragmatist. He wants Francis to leave
> his mop and help his candidate.*

> *Lobby of the downtown Washington, DC, office building where
> Francis works. It is night. Francis, in custodial uniform, works an
> electric buffer machine.*

FRANCIS: "The world has never had a good definition of the word liberty,
and the American people, just now, are in much want of one. We all
declare for liberty; in using the same word, we do not all mean the
same thing. With some, the word liberty may mean for each man to
do as he pleases with himself and the product of his labor; while
with others the word may mean for men to do as they please with
other men, and the product of other men's labor. Each of these
things is called by two different and incompatible names — liberty
and tyranny.
*(Enter somewhat cautiously a lawyer-type, middle-aged, with the req-
uisite briefcase and conservative suit. This is Harold Daly, lawyer-
lobbyist-image shaper. He may have been eavesdropping.)*

DALY: Hey.
(Francis halts the machine, freezes.)

DALY: Doing a heck of a job on that floor. You can see your face in it.
*(A beat. Francis restarts the machine, continues buffing, avoiding eye
contact with the man.)*

DALY: You're new here. Aren't you? In the building? . . . You know, you
remind me of someone. I don't suppose we've met before?

(Francis shuts off the machine. A beat.)

FRANCIS: No.

DALY: Lobby's never looked better. *(An introduction.)* Hoffman, Sanders, Daly. Fifth and sixth floors. I'm Daly.

FRANCIS: Harold Daly. The papers call you "the king of the king-makers."

DALY: Among other things. What's your name?

FRANCIS: I, sir, am . . . *(This takes an effort.)* I'm Francis.

DALY: Francis. They've got you on the night shift.

FRANCIS: Yes.

DALY: You and I might be the only workers left in the building at this hour.

FRANCIS: I prefer it. The quiet.

DALY: You know something? I do, too. I think I'm becoming more of a loner as I get older.

FRANCIS: Contemplation befits the later years.

DALY: *(A beat.)* Would you say that again for me?

FRANCIS: "Contemplation befits the later years."

DALY: I thought that's what I heard. Francis. Mind if I run something by you? Get your opinion. My firm does lobbying, public opinion research — among other things. We lawyers get bogged down in detail, lose the big picture. I find it helpful to hear from the man in the street, so to speak.

FRANCIS: *(Being witty.)* Or the buffer in the lobby.

DALY: *(Appreciating it.)* That's right. So here's the issue. Let's see what you think. Excessive pay for corporate execs. You know, multiple millions in salary, sweetheart stock deals, etc. Let's say you're a congressman — in fact, you're one of my boys. You take a huge amount of money from these overpaid execs. But polls show that voters overwhelmingly think it's bad. So your take on it is, it's bad. *(Quickly here, the salesman with a pitch.)* But. Over-compensated CEOs actually project a positive corporate image of prosperity and healthy cash reserves, so overcompensation is a sort of controlled excess that encourages a free-market economy, reinforces the vital infrastructure of American democracy and gives the nation's kids something to shoot for, what do you think?

FRANCIS: Labyrinthine.

DALY: Say again?

FRANCIS: Excessive pay is bad because it is wrong. The matter is simple. Complicating it is dishonest. For the orator, the last, best hope of persuasion lies in the simple.

DALY: *(Searching for a pen.)* Could you . . . ? Do you mind if I jot that down? "The last, best hope of persuasion . . ." That's good. What do you think the people want, Francis? In general. Off the top of your head.

FRANCIS: Inspiration.

DALY: Not money? Security? Health insurance?

FRANCIS: Temporal and corporal satisfaction are never equal to satisfaction of the spirit.

DALY: Right . . . It's funny you say that. I heard a speech the other night. Congressman. Guy named Carpenter. He's running against our client. I have to admit, it was actually inspiring. Never heard anything like it.

FRANCIS: Yes you have.

DALY: It gave me a shiver. How many speeches by a politician these days give you a shiver?

FRANCIS: Precious few.

DALY: And this guy Carpenter is such a loser. My job is to break him down into bite-size chunks, chew him up and spit out the bones. You follow politics?

FRANCIS: Some.

DALY: We've got his bank records, medical records, college transcripts, family history — there's a disgraceful embarrassment in there somewhere. Has to be. Rules of the game.

FRANCIS: You sound worried, Mister Daly.

DALY: Do I? Have you always been a floor buffer, Francis?

FRANCIS: No.

DALY: No, I didn't think so. Where'd you go to school?

FRANCIS: I had little formal education.

DALY: Self-taught?

FRANCIS: Largely. I attended a one-room schoolhouse as a child.

DALY: Seriously?

FRANCIS: Oh yes.

DALY: I didn't think they had those anymore. How did you wind up polishing the floor in my lobby?

FRANCIS: I suffered a disappointment.

DALY: Really.

FRANCIS: Yes.

DALY: Tell me about it.

FRANCIS: I can't.

DALY: *(A beat; respectfully.)* Francis? Can I try that thing? *(The buffer.)*

FRANCIS: This?

DALY: Yeah.

FRANCIS: Here. Stand firm. Let the machine do the work all around you. *(Daly turns on the machine, buffs happily for a moment.)*

DALY: Look at that shine . . . This is the most useful thing I've done all day . . . Manual labor. Frees up your mind.

FRANCIS: Yes.

DALY: At home I used to mow. Same kind of thing. Loved it. But my wife hired landscapers. Said she was worried about my heart. But she wasn't.

FRANCIS: No?

DALY: No. Pure malice. She saw I enjoyed it. So she took it away. She's a very unhappy person.

FRANCIS: I am sorry to learn it.

DALY: Yeah.

FRANCIS: What is the cause of your wife's unhappiness?

DALY: Me.

FRANCIS: Then might you not also be the remedy?

DALY: *(He thinks about that.)* We're probably beyond remedies. You know why I stay late at the office most nights, Francis?

FRANCIS: No.

DALY: I don't want to go home. *(He stops the machine.)* I don't love my wife anymore. I haven't loved her for ten years. I don't have the courage to say it to her.

FRANCIS: I suspect, sir, that you say it every evening with your late arrival home.

DALY: Why doesn't she answer me, then?

FRANCIS: Perhaps she does so — with her malice, as you put it.

DALY: We've stayed together mostly because of the girls, but they're both married now, so what's the point anymore? We've wounded each other so many times. Scars on top of scars.

FRANCIS: Two armies aligned against one another. One side charges, the other falls back, then counters. No decisive blow is struck, so the battle continues endlessly, until fighting becomes its own excuse for more fighting.

DALY: So how do we stop?

FRANCIS: The greater courage now is in diplomacy.

DALY: No, we've talked and talked. It always turns into an argument. Sometimes I think about just packing it all up and going away. Did you ever feel that way?

FRANCIS: There's abundant land in the western territories.

DALY: Just jump in the car and drive till I come to a place that looks like where I'd want to start over.

FRANCIS: Springfield, Illinois.

DALY: I'd look for some place small and quiet. Where a man can cut his own damn grass.

FRANCIS: Invite your spouse to go with you.

DALY: What? No. she'll be glad to see me go.

FRANCIS: Allow yourself the opportunity to be surprised.

DALY: *(He ponders that a moment. Sadly.)* You know, Francis, I got more pleasure out of shining this floor than anything I've done in a month.

FRANCIS: What if you were to say to her, I wish to love you as fully as I once did. And ask her if she too does not wish to love as fully.

DALY: She'll laugh at me. She'll think I've gone crazy.

FRANCIS: Go crazy, Mister Daly. In a city so desperately sane, crazy is the remedy.

DALY: Francis. Call me Harry.

FRANCIS: Harry. Call me — *(He has to think about this for a beat.)* Would you be willing to call me Abe?

DALY: "Abe"?

FRANCIS: Just for tonight. If you have no objection.

DALY: Abe it is. Will you do me a favor, Abe? I'd like the pleasure of buying you a drink.

FRANCIS: I am forbidden to drink. And I have work still to do.

DALY: I own this building. And I say you've done enough work on it tonight.

(Lights. Transition.)

MAURITIUS

Theresa Rebeck

Dramatic
Dennis, thirties; Sterling, forties to fifties

> *While hanging out in a philately shop Dennis has discovered what might be the world's rarest stamp, in a collection brought in for appraisal by a young woman who has absolutely no idea what she has. Sterling is a rather shady collector and investor, and Dennis hopes to broker a deal for him to buy the stamp.*

> *Dennis and Sterling, in a coffee shop.*

STERLING: I don't believe you.

DENNIS: I saw it.

STERLING: You saw it.

DENNIS: Yes. I touched it.

STERLING: You touched it.

DENNIS: *(Firm.)* Yes I did.

STERLING: I don't believe you.

DENNIS: I don't care if you believe me or not. I half don't believe it myself.

> *(They think for a moment.)*

STERLING: It's a fake.

DENNIS: It's not a fake.

STERLING: You only saw it for a second.

DENNIS: He was right over my shoulder! What was I supposed to do?

STERLING: Shit. Fuck. I don't believe you.

DENNIS: Fuck you.

> *(Beat.)*

STERLING: So this person just walked in, opened a book, and showed it to you.

DENNIS: Yes!

STERLING: What kind of shape was it in?

DENNIS: Uncancelled, it looks like it may have been previously slip mounted but other than the barest memory of that slip mount, along the barest sliver of it's border, I would have to say that it is . . . pristine.

STERLING: Fuck, that's . . .

DENNIS: I saw it!

STERLING: And then she went home?

DENNIS: She did.

STERLING: She walked in, and walked out, you let her just walk out with it?

DENNIS: Well, I followed her.

STERLING: Where'd she go?

DENNIS: She went home.

STERLING: Where?

DENNIS: Oh no no. No no no.

STERLING: This story is shit. You think I don't know when I'm being played?

DENNIS: I think you do know when you're being played, Sterling, which is why you're still sitting here.

STERLING: Fuck you, you little piece of shit. You bring me this fucking preposterous story about some girl with a — fuck you. *Fuck you.* Life is short my friend, and it's getting shorter, you bring stories like this to the table. You ask yourself, what do you want out of life? I advise you.

　　At moments like this, you are stepping out over the abyss, for what? How much money is it worth to you, Dennis, to risk what will befall you, I don't say possibly, I say certainly, what will befall a person like you, stepping onto the highwire of complete bullshit that just came out of your mouth.

DENNIS: How much do I want? Is that what you just asked me? How much money do I expect you to pay me to make this happen?
(Beat, happy.)
A lot, Sterling. Really, quite a lot.
(Beat.)

STERLING: You're lying, or she is.

DENNIS: I'm not lying. And she doesn't know how to lie.

STERLING: Since you spent so much time with her. And you know her so well.

DENNIS: She reads comic books, Sterling. This girl is a lamb.

(A beat, while Sterling considers.)

STERLING: I don't believe you. I'm leaving.

(He stands to go. Dennis leans back in his chair, lets him get all the way across the room, then calls after him.)

DENNIS: I didn't tell you everything.

(Sterling stops, but doesn't turn.)

DENNIS: *(Continuing.)* There are two of them. The one penny *and* the two penny.

(Sterling turns and looks at Dennis. Dennis shrugs, laughs. He is very happy. Blackout.)

STEVE AND IDI
David Grimm

Dramatic
Steve, thirties; Brad, twenties

> *Steve, a gay man, is so lonely that he has resorted to calling a gay "escort service." Brad is the handsome young man they have sent over to his apartment. Brad has fallen for Steve (or at least he says he has), which is not exactly what Steve had in mind.*

> *Night. The room is empty and dimly lit. A different donut is on the TV set. Brad enters from the bedroom in a jockstrap.*

BRAD: Through here?
> *(Brad exits into the bathroom. Pause. The sound of a shower running. Steve enters from the bedroom in a bathrobe, carrying Brad's clothes. He puts these on an armchair. He sits on the couch, pours and drinks a shot of vodka, lost in thought.)*
> *(Pause.)*
> *(He dials his cell phone. Waits. Getting voice mail, he hangs up.)*
> *(The shower switches off. The sound of pebbles hitting the windowpane. Steve goes to the window and looks out. Nothing.)*

BRAD: *(Off.)* Hey, I love your shower.
> *(Brad re-enters from the bathroom, wet and wearing a towel. As he speaks, Brad sits on the couch and proceeds to cut a couple lines of coke.)* Awesome water pressure. Seriously. My shower sucks. I'm four floors up and by the time it gets there — You can stand under it for hours and pfft — !

STEVE: I brought out your clothes.
> *(Brad snorts two lines of coke.)*

BRAD: You want some more?
> *(Steve does a line.)*
> Hey —

(Brad kisses Steve.)

You got a great place. Feels really homey. Hey, you know you got a donut up here?

STEVE: What?

BRAD: *(Picking up the donut and biting into it before Steve can respond:)* Mind if I — ?

STEVE: . . . Oh Jesus.

BRAD: Yeah, you should see my place. Like a fuckin' shoebox in a sewer, only smaller. It's got this stain on the wall when you walk in — I don't know if it's dry rot or where someone shot their brains out. This is a Krispy Kreme, isn't it? I can tell. My brother, he loves Dunkin' Donuts, but I'm a Krispy Kreme man myself.

STEVE: It's a sign.

BRAD: I know, right? By the way, I should warn you: I'm a Gemini, but that's a whole other thing. So anyway, this stain: my landlord won't fix it. Says it looks like the Virgin Mary. She's Dominican and a total Sagittarius. Hey, has anyone ever told you you look like that actor-dude, what's-his-name —

STEVE: Yeah him.

BRAD: Man, you don't even know who I'm talking about. You do. You know how sometimes when you look at someone all up close, like when you're kissing them, they look all different?

STEVE: Listen, I'm sorry but I'm really fading here.

BRAD: Do another line.

STEVE: It's not that. I —

BRAD: Bet I know how to wake you up.

(Brad kisses Steve. Steve tries to laugh it off.)

STEVE: Sorry, I'm really —

BRAD: You don't really want me to go, do you?

STEVE: *(Pause.)* I have a really early morning tomorrow.

(Awkward pause.)

BRAD: Hey. It's cool.

(Brad dresses.)

I'm not usually — It's this time of year, you know? Winter in the big city. Everyone all bundled up in their little lives, running around like rats. Not exactly "It's a Wonderful Life." Gets kinda — You know? I mean I don't really usually hook up a lot and — I don't know, you wanna get together again sometime, or —

STEVE: *(Lying.)* Sure. No, that would be cool.

BRAD: Sweet. Maybe next week?

STEVE: Well, you have my screen name, so —

BRAD: Right. Cool.

Very cool indeed.

Hey, you are negative, right?

STEVE: What?

BRAD: Your status. You're negative, right?

STEVE: Isn't that a bit cart before the horse asking that now?

BRAD: How'd you mean?

STEVE: Closing the barn door after the — Never mind. Yes, I'm negative.

BRAD: Very cool. Me too.

Ever do bareback?

STEVE: No.

BRAD: Yeah, me neither.

Would be hot though.

(Going in for a kiss:) Well, it was nice to —

STEVE: When were you last tested, Brad? It is Brad, isn't it?

BRAD: Yeah.

STEVE: When were you last tested? For HIV.

BRAD: Me? Oh I haven't been tested. I just know I'm negative.

STEVE: Wow. You a gypsy fortune teller?

BRAD: No. Italian.,

STEVE: Never mind.

BRAD: *(Pause. Smiling.)* I like you.

I don't really get you, but I like you, you know? I have this sense.

I'm good at reading people. You really do — You look like that —

STEVE: *(Gently.)* You really shouldn't speak.

I'm sorry, I just don't want to know you.

BRAD: *(Pause. Cold.)* Yeah. OK.

OK.

(Steve shows Brad to the door and holds it open.)

STEVE: Good night.

BRAD: You know what? Fuck you.

STEVE: Excuse me?

BRAD: You heard me, man. Fuck you. I thought we had a pretty hot time, you know? I thought there was a — you know — a-a connection. I mean, it wasn't just in my head, right? Is it so wrong to want — Why's it such a fucking crime to be honest with someone and want a little — Oh forget it. Typical faggot shit. Who needs it. Fuckin' loser.

(Brad exits. Steve remains holding the door open, stunned.)

(From off:) Fuckin' loser!

(Steve slowly closes the door. He stands there for a moment.)

STEVE: *(To himself; Mocking.)* I'm a Krispy Kreme man myself.

TRUMPERY

Peter Parnell

Dramatic
Darwin, sixties; Wallace, thirties to forties

> *Charles Darwin has delayed publication of his "Origin of Species"*
> *for 20 years for fear of the firestorm it will create, but he may have*
> *to publish the book at last because a younger acolyte named Wallace*
> *has, independently, come up with the same theories as Darwin's.*
> *Here, they meet for the first time.*
>
> *Wallace sits down beside Darwin. Puts his arms around him.*
> *Darwin looks at Wallace.*

DARWIN: Earthworms. I've been studying them. To see if they exhibit
signs of natural selection. I've been trying to train them. But it's difficult, you know, because they can neither see nor hear.

WALLACE: Slow pupils.

DARWIN: No pupils, actually. They are feisty creatures, however. Their
persistence fills me with admiration.

(Pause.)

WALLACE: When we look around us here, at this very beautiful garden,
we know it is a jungle, a battleground for survival. But we alone can
also admire its beauty. We alone have an appreciation of higher
things. Does that include our moral sense? And with it, our sense of
community? In this regard, are we not like that bee hive, which
works together for the common good —

DARWIN: On the contrary, if we were reared as hive bees, our unmarried
females would think it a sacred duty to kill their brothers, our
mothers would try to kill their fertile daughters, and no one would
think of interfering!

WALLACE: Nevertheless, our moral faculties are higher. We are both of
this garden, and outside it. Beyond it, even. Whether Man is

beyond natural selection or not, where will what is good for our own survival as a species lead us?

(Pause.)

Everything I see around me since coming back home to England — our factories, our capitalism — shows us that the fittest survive. But in order for our species to survive, we must — and our very biology knows that we must — cooperate. Not fight. Mutual aid, Charles. Altruism. It is not to the individual, but to the tribe that we must look. It is what is good for the race that will win out, over what is good for the individual. These are my personal beliefs, but they are also my scientific ones.

(Pause.)

We are at the dawn of a wonderful age, Charles. In the new century, everyone will work out his own happiness. Man will know how to govern himself, there will be voluntary associations for the public good, and natural selection will lead, finally, to a truly free and egalitarian society.

DARWIN: Utopian nonsense. Nature is devoid of such lofty ideals . . . and men . . . like all the other animals . . . are mere barnacles, fumbling over on top of each other . . . in the dark!

(Pause.)

Did you know that the sun is cooling? Fairly rapidly, according to that physicist Thomson. Which means the earth will, inescapably, freeze. To think of the progress of millions of years of evolution, and of the struggles of countless men, to lead to that!

(Pause.)

I do comfort myself a little. When someone writes to tell me I have confirmed his belief that the Universe was not the result of chance, I tell him I no longer know what I believe, or care. What does it matter? What does a monkey believe about chance? Our minds will continue to evolve, and with it our beliefs. It prevents having to be convinced of ANYTHING anymore!

(Pause.)

I'm sorry. For what I did. I killed all three of you. God. Annie. You.

WALLACE: Killed us? What are you talking about?

DARWIN: Twenty years. An entire life's work. Do you think I could let it all go? Hooker warned me. He warned me I would be forestalled. And then, when it happened, when it actually — To think of all my originality smashed — Did you think I would *not* fight to claim priority? Who would not fight? I protect my theories like I protect my children!

WALLACE: Our babies. Our theories. Terrible when they are lost.

(Pause.)

DARWIN: Are you going to fight, Wallace? Claim I stole from you?

WALLACE: Fight? Why would I fight? Charles — there is nothing to fight about. I couldn't have written your book. I could never have done the job you did.

DARWIN: But the *idea* —

WALLACE: The important thing is not who has the idea, but who figures out what to do with it.

(Pause.)

All our work must be a true collaboration. It only proves my latest belief, which is what I want to write about.

(Pause.)

I want to thank you, Charles.

DARWIN: Thank me?

WALLACE: I came here to find out what happened. I have wanted to know, for the longest time, exactly how the theory came to be called the Darwin-Wallace theory. I felt — and now it's confirmed — that you were being very generous to me.

DARWIN: Generous . . . ?

WALLACE: Yes. For putting my essay together with yours — you, who had worked so hard, as you had told me, all those years before. I felt, after hearing what happened, as though I had accomplished nothing. I simply wanted to know: *Did I help?*

DARWIN: Help . . . ? Wallace. I couldn't have published without you!

(Pause.)

(Wallace smiles.)

WALLACE: Exactly. And that pleases me. I am glad how it has turned out.

(Pause.)

DARWIN: I am sorry, Wallace. I believe I have misjudged you. Once you view the world as a place of harsh competition, you feel you must engage in it the same way. Can you not understand what that has done to me?

(Pause.)

The plain truth is, your cockeyed idealism has saved you. You may have discovered survival of the fittest, but what you have done with it has made, for you, all the difference. What you have come to discover about the world, about life, has made you happy. What I have discovered about the world has made me sad. The funny part is, a few quibbles aside, we both discovered the exact same thing . . .

WALLACE: And isn't that extraordinary? *(Quotes:)* "Thus, from the war of nature, from famine and death, the most exalted object which we are capable of conceiving, namely, the production of the higher animals, directly follows . . ."

DARWIN: ". . . There is grandeur in this view of life . . . and whilst this planet has gone cycling on according to the fixed law of gravity, from so simple a beginning endless forms most beautiful and wonderful have been, and are being evolved . . ."

(Pause.)

WALLACE: How powerful you think you are, Charles! And yet, how small! How painful to feel guilt. And yet how much more reassuring than to feel despair! Why not try and take comfort, Charles, in the fact that there is so much even you cannot control. For you, like the rest of us, are, finally, only human . . .

DARWIN: *(Quietly.)* Trumpery.

WALLACE: What?

DARWIN: No. Nothing.

WALLACE: And now, Charles, you must write about Man. We must BOTH write about Man. But first, we should try and get some sleep.

(Darwin scoops the earth.)

DARWIN: The worms. Soon, we shall all be food for them. They will digest us to be renewed. And we will become part of the earth, and reborn again in it. And that, Wallace, may well be the most marvelous thing of all. . .

WITTENBERG
David Davalos

Comic
Luther and Faustus, forties to fifties

> *Martin Luther has come to his old friend Dr. Faustus for a medical physical.*

> *Scene: Faustus' study. Faustus examines Luther, initially with his ear against Luther's belly.*

LUTHER: When was your last confession?

FAUSTUS: When was your last check-up?

LUTHER: I worry about your soul.

FAUSTUS: I worry about your bowels.

LUTHER: I've tried and I've tried but nothing is forthcoming.

FAUSTUS: How long?

LUTHER: Six days.

FAUSTUS: O, Martin, come on. God made the universe in six days. I don't think you're really trying.

LUTHER: I'm trying!

FAUSTUS: Are the headaches back?

LUTHER: Yes, of course . . . my head is throbbing even now.

FAUSTUS: Describe the pain.

LUTHER: The same as always. A metal band clamped around my head. Thorns at my temples. I can hear the movement of my blood. On the nights I sleep, I wake up feeling like someone's hammered a rusty iron spike into the back of my head.

FAUSTUS: How deep does the spike go?

LUTHER: To just behind my eyes.

FAUSTUS: What are you eating?

LUTHER: The usual. Liver. Cabbage. Limburger.

FAUSTUS: The occasional Body-of-Christ.

LUTHER: Yes, if you have to put it that way.

FAUSTUS: It wasn't my idea. What are you drinking?

LUTHER: What is there to drink? Milk, beer, water, beer.

FAUSTUS: Blood-of-Christ at least twice a week.

LUTHER: Damn it, John —

FAUSTUS: A glass a day is actually good for the heart. So: angsty, much? Any particular sturm blowing? Any source of Drang?

LUTHER: Well, that damned Tetzel . . .

FAUSTUS: Tetzel?

LUTHER: John Tetzel, John! Tetzel! Dominican huckster, selling indulgences like lottery tickets. My flock no longer comes to confession! They have no cause to repent! They believe they've already purchased their salvation from the Church, and have the holy receipt to prove it! They're actually being told they can buy their way out of all their sins committed and those yet to commit! Ridiculous! Tetzel! Shearing the sheep!

FAUSTUS: I take it you have a theological dispute with Tetzel.

LUTHER: I have a theological dispute with the entire idea of it!

FAUSTUS: Martin! Heresy! Good for you!

LUTHER: What? No, no . . .

FAUSTUS: And what are you doing about it?

LUTHER: What am I doing about it?

FAUSTUS: What are you doing about it?

LUTHER: I'm not doing anything about it!

FAUSTUS: You're not doing anything about it. Well, there's your problem, Martin. There's your blockage. My diagnosis is, you're literally full of shit. It's backed up all the way to your brain in the form of a rusty iron spike.

LUTHER: Useless. You're useless.

FAUSTUS: Seems like it's pressing on the free-will portion of your brain, inhibiting it.

LUTHER: You're a quack.

FAUSTUS: But I do have a treatment. Part pharmacological, part occupational.

LUTHER: Just kill me now.

(Faustus prepares Luther's medication of ground beans.)

FAUSTUS: The pharmacological part is a little something I smuggled out of Mecca over the summer.

LUTHER: O, perfect. Foreign poison.

FAUSTUS: You really need to get out more, you bumpkin.

LUTHER: Wittenberg is world enough for me.

FAUSTUS: "The world is a book, and those who do not travel read only a page."

LUTHER: Yes, yes, don't quote Augustine to an Augustinian.

FAUSTUS: When he's right, he's right. But only when he's right. Behold, magic beans. Grind 'em up, they make a kind of musclebound tea — recommended for headaches, constipation and the general defluxion of humours. It also has the effect of stimulating the attention and increasing mental speed; my colleague Abdullah says it puts the whirl in your dervish and the fizz in your fez. It's called "qahfe," and to the Sultans, it is "the milk of chess players and thinkers." Just mix with water and boil.

LUTHER: I'm not drinking any hellfired heathen shitwater.

FAUSTUS: You'll drink what I tell you to drink if you don't want to explode. And you'll drink three cups of it a day: two at Matins, one at Nones. Unclench, Martin. You're going to like it. It'll keep you awake for all that praying you have to do. Trust me: stick with it for a week, and the problem will be getting you *off* the stuff.

LUTHER: Does it go with eggs?

FAUSTUS: It goes with everything. Secondly, I want you to make it an exercise to sit down and write a little every day.

LUTHER: What? No . . .

FAUSTUS: It can be on any topic you like, but at least one page a day.

LUTHER: I don't have time for this . . .

FAUSTUS: I'm just asking you to cut out fifteen minutes of flesh-mortification and sit down with a quill and parchment. I think you'll find the words will come.

LUTHER: I have nothing to write about. . .

FAUSTUS: O, no? Shall I give you a topic for the first day? All right, let's see . . . the topic is Tetzel.

LUTHER: Tetzel!

FAUSTUS: Tetzel. Write a page about Tetzel.

LUTHER: Tetzel. Profanity acceptable?

FAUSTUS: Use any language you like. It's not for publication.

LUTHER: Tetzel. Anything else?

FAUSTUS: The qahfe and the quill, and that's it. Give the qahfe twenty-four hours, and if it's not producing the desired effects, we'll try it in another orifice.

LUTHER: What?

FAUSTUS: Remember, a page a day is only the minimum. Write as much as you like. There might be more than a page in Tetzel.

LUTHER: Tetzel. I'll see you in confession on Sunday?

FAUSTUS: Well . . .

LUTHER: I'll see you in confession on Sunday!

FAUSTUS: Ah, that Luther charm. Look, Helen's back in town tomorrow. Finally. My appointment book will be full for the next few days.

LUTHER: For the record, I am obligated to object to that . . . relationship.

FAUSTUS: What does that mean, obligated?

LUTHER: The Church teaches it's a sin. You're sinning. With a sinner. Sinfully. I am forbidden to condone it.

FAUSTUS: You're forbidden?

LUTHER: I am bound by my vows.

FAUSTUS: You're vow-bound?

LUTHER: Stop that! What do you want me to say? I'm trying to be delicate. She's a fallen woman — you should know, because you pushed her. And then you jumped down after her. Into a pool of sin. I have professional reservations.

FAUSTUS: A pool of sin? Come on in, the water's fine. A pool of sin. Well, we're drying off. When next I see her, I'm going to pose the question.

LUTHER: You're going to marry that woman?

FAUSTUS: Joined in the eyes of the Lord.

LUTHER: In a church?

FAUSTUS: Well, that is where they keep the sanctimony.

LUTHER: The sanctity.

FAUSTUS: O, right, sure — sorry I still don't know my sanctorum from a hole in the ground.

LUTHER: I can actually feel my patience evaporating.

FAUSTUS: I can actually smell it. Truthfully, I was hoping you would perform the ceremony.

LUTHER: Me? Marry you?

FAUSTUS: O, Martin, I'm flattered, but I'm sure the Church wouldn't approve.

LUTHER: Is this the pretext for another practical joke?

FAUSTUS: I'm hurt. Really. Where is your faith? It's real, it's true . . . What can I tell you — I'm helpless, it's love.

LUTHER: Hmph. It's a kind of love, perhaps.

FAUSTUS: Every love is a kind of love. "Let the root of love be within, for of this root can nothing spring but what is good."

LUTHER: Yes, and Augustine also said, "Love is the beauty of the soul." You see? It always comes back to the soul, you miscreant. The marriage ceremony is part of a package deal. It comes with communion, and it comes with confession. And I can only pray there might follow an appropriate lifestyle change. You need to accept that it's a matter of your immortal soul, which is never beyond redemption, John, no matter how hard you may try. "Sin couches at the door; its urge is toward you, yet you can be its master."

FAUSTUS: Sin's here already? She's early.

LUTHER: Listen, jackass, if you and your . . . counterpart are serious about this, then take it seriously. I'm serious! Meantime, I'll be praying for you. To Saint Jude, I fear, but praying all the same, damn it. Praying hard.

FAUSTUS: Sure, in lieu of cash, just put your treatment on the divine tab. Pray-as-you-go medicine.

(Luther heads out.)

Aren't you even going to congratulate me?

LUTHER: Congratulations. With qualifications.

FAUSTUS: I wouldn't expect it any other way, you sentimental little girl.

LUTHER: Impertinent.

FAUSTUS: Dyspeptic.

LUTHER: Dilettante!

FAUSTUS: Drudge!

LUTHER: Save your soul, John.

FAUSTUS: Free your mind, Martin.

(Exit Luther, lights down on Faustus.)

Scenes for Two Women

AMERICAN GIRLS
Hilary Bettis

Seriocomic
Katie and Amanda, teens

> *Katie and Amanda, two middle-school girls, have entered a "talent competition" which they thought would result in their becoming Hollywood stars. This competition turns out to be extremely sleazy. Here, they are in the ladies' room, trying to decide if they are gonna go through with performing.*

> *Lights up on a small, disgusting bathroom. Katie and Amanda scamper in. Music underneath.*

AMANDA: Ohmigod, ohmigod! Do you think she touched me?

KATIE: I don't know!

AMANDA: Ewwww I think she touched me —

KATIE: Ohmigosh I am so freaked out right now!

Did you see the way she was staring at us?

AMANDA: She wasn't staring at me, she was staring at you!

KATIE: I'm so freaked out! I've never been around a lesbian before —

AMANDA: Katie!

KATIE: Shut up!

AMANDA: Sorry. I mean Virginia!

KATIE: What?

AMANDA: You shouldn't say things like that about people you don't know!

KATIE: Then you go back out there and change in front of her!

AMANDA: No way!

KATIE: Then don't get mad at me for saying she's a lesbo —

AMANDA: You don't know —

KATIE: I overheard one of the girls tell another girl that the weird girl is a lesbian and has AIDS. That's why her face looks all scarred with all those purple marks. Why would someone lie about something like that? They wouldn't! I'm just looking out for our best interest!

AMANDA: Shut up! What if she hears you? And then she tries to come in here and be a lesbo with us and then we get AIDS!

KATIE: What if we already have it?

AMANDA: Will you stop talking about it! You are freaking me out. She doesn't have AIDS. I can tell she doesn't have it so relax and shut up!

KATIE: I don't think we should be doing this —

AMANDA: You wanna chicken out on me?

KATIE: No, I didn't say that, I just . . .

AMANDA: This is our one adventure. We are in this together. If there's really a Hollywood talent scout out there this could be how we get discovered. What are you scared of?

KATIE: I don't know.

AMANDA: This is how I look at it. We dance all the time right? In our bedrooms, and ballet lessons when we were five, and even at school dances. I mean at the last dance we had at school all the girls were wearing short skirts and just as much makeup as we are now and tight shirts and I mean, you didn't even wear a bra Virginia. And we were cheerleaders in Middle School and we're gonna try out for cheerleading in high school and they wear short skirts and kick their legs in front of boys so everyone can see up their skirts. So what is the difference between dancing there and here? Nothing. That is what girls do. It is the way God made us and Jesus would not have made us as hot as we are if He didn't have a plan for us. Seriously, we would be like blasphemizing Him if we didn't do this. If we get famous then we can spread the word of the Lord and isn't that ultimately what we should be doing?

KATIE: Of course.

AMANDA: So don't you think that we owe it to our Savior and to the plan He has for us to do this?

KATIE: Yes. Alright, yes!

(A pause.)

KATIE: I wish Rob could see me.

AMANDA: Ohmigod will you shut up about Rob for like five seconds?

KATIE: I didn't even say anything!

(Katie pulls off her clothes. She has a very sexy and grown-up teddy on.)

AMANDA: I love that teddy on you! It makes you look like a playboy model.

KATIE: Really?

AMANDA: I really love your boobs.

KATIE: You do? I think they're gross.

AMANDA: They're not! Guys love them! At least you have boobs, I don't have anything! If I don't get bigger boobs by tenth grade, I'm saving up for a boob job! I want them like this big! Then I'll shake them in your face!

(Amanda shakes her chest in Katie's face.)

KATIE: Ohmigod, get those mosquito bites out of my face before I bite them off!

AMANDA: I heard if a girl has cold hands then she is good in bed.

KATIE: How do you know that?

AMANDA: I heard it on MTV.

KATIE: I have cold hands all the time!

AMANDA: So do I, but I wear gloves.

KATIE: You're so dumb.

AMANDA: This is just between you and me right?

KATIE: Cross my heart and hope to die. Stick a needle in my eye. Pinky swear with spit!

(The girls spit on their pinkies and shake. The girls exit.)

THE BEEBO BRINKER CHRONICLES

Kate Moira Ryan and Linda S. Chapman

Seriocomic
Beebo and Laura, twenties to thirties

> *This play takes place in the repressed 1950s, in Greenwich Village.*
> *Laura, a sensitive Midwesterner, has fled to NYC to try to get over*
> *a failed romance with a woman who has married a man instead.*
> *She meets Beebo, an extremely aggressive woman who is trying to*
> *pick her up.*

> *The Cellar. Laura orders a drink. Beebo walks in and sits down*
> *next to her.*

LAURA: Here's your dime Beebo. Next time don't waste your money.

BEEBO: I always get what I pay for lover. What's the matter Laura afraid
to look at me?

LAURA: Laura's not afraid of you or anyone else.

BEEBO: Where's your guardian angel tonight?

LAURA: I suppose you mean Jack. I called him. He's entertaining. Maybe
he'll meet me, maybe he won't. I'm a big girl.

BEEBO: Oh, excuse me, I should have noticed.

LAURA: You only see what you want to see.

BEEBO: I see what I want to see right now.

LAURA: Go away. Leave me alone.

BEEBO: What's the matter little girl, hate the world? Let me guess you're
unlucky in love or you just found out that you're gay. Or is it sweet
sixteen and never been kissed?

LAURA: I'm twenty.

BEEBO: Excuse me. Twenty. Your innocence is getting tedious lover.

LAURA: Beebo I don't like you. I don't like the way you dress. Or the way you talk, or the way you do your hair. I don't want your dimes and I don't want you. I hope that's plain because I don't know how to make it any plainer.

(Begins to sob.)

BEEBO: Tell me baby. Tell me all about it.

LAURA: I can't I can't tell you or anybody.

BEEBO: Try baby. Try.

LAURA: It's stupid; it's ridiculous. We're complete strangers.

BEEBO: You don't need to tell me about it, because I already know. I've lived through it too. You fall in love. You're young, you're inexperienced. You fall, up to your ears and there's nobody to talk to, nobody to lean on. You're all alone with that great big miserable feeling and she's driving you out of your mind. Finally you give in to it and she's straight. End of story. End of soap opera. And then again, beginning of soap opera. That's all the village is honey, just one crazy little soap opera after another. All tangled up with each other, one piled on top of the next, ad infinitum Mary loves Jean, Jane loves Joan, Joan loves Jean and Beebo loves Laura. Doesn't mean a thing. It goes on forever. Where one stops another begins. I know most of the girls in here. I've probably slept with half of them, I've lived with half of the half I've slept with. What does it all come to? You know something baby? It doesn't matter. Nothing matters. You don't like me and that doesn't matter. Someday maybe you'll love me, and that won't matter either. Because it won't last. Not down here. Not anywhere in the world, if you're gay you'll never find peace, you'll never find Love. With a capital L. L for Love. L for Laura. L for Lust and L for the L of it. L for Lesbian. L for let's, let's. Let's. How about it? Want to go home with Beebo?

LAURA: Beebo. Where did you get that ridiculous name?

BEEBO: My family.

LAURA: They named you Beebo?

BEEBO: Worse. They named me Betty Jean. Even Mother couldn't stand it. That's why they called me Beebo.

LAURA: What's your last name?

BEEBO: Brinker. Like the silver skates.

(Laura counts out her change.)

You're a dime short of another drink. Want your dime back?

LAURA: I don't want to owe you a thing.

BEEBO: How are you going to get home? Or do you want to get home. It must have been a bad fight.

LAURA: It wasn't a fight.

BEEBO: She straight?

LAURA: Yes, she's straight.

BEEBO: Did you tell her about yourself?

LAURA: I don't know if I did or didn't, but I acted like a fool.

BEEBO: If she's straight it's hopeless.

LAURA: That's what Jack says.

BEEBO: Jack's right.

LAURA: He's not in love with her.

BEEBO: Get out while you can.

LAURA: I can't.

BEEBO: Go home and get your heart broken. It's the only way to learn, I guess.

LAURA: *(Grabs Beebo's wrist.)* I can't go home. Not tonight.

BEEBO: Come home with me. Come on sweetie pie. I'm a nice kid, I won't eat you.

THE BEEBO BRINKER CHRONICLES

Kate Moira Ryan and London S. Chapman

Seriocomic
Beebo and Laura, twenties to thirties

> *This play takes place in the repressed 1950s, in Greenwich Village.*
> *Laura, a sensitive Midwesterner, has fled to NYC to try to get over*
> *a failed romance with a woman, Beth, who has married a man*
> *instead. She has been sleeping with Beebo, who has just found out*
> *that Laura's heart belongs to Beth.*

BEEBO: Who's Beth?

LAURA: Beth? Where are my clothes?

BEEBO: Is Beth your roommate?

LAURA: No, my roommate is Marcie.

BEEBO: Baby, it seems it's Beth you're after not Marcie.

LAURA: Beth is married. It's over.

BEEBO: It's over for her maybe.

LAURA: Where are my clothes, Beebo?

BEEBO: Did you enjoy yourself last night? After all it was your idea, baby.
You crawled into my bed.

LAURA: I couldn't help myself last night. It's been such a long time.

BEEBO: Since Beth?

LAURA: I acted like a fool with my roommate.

BEEBO: So you came down here. Let off some steam. And there I was
ready and willing. What would you have done if I turned you
down?

LAURA: I don't know.

BEEBO: I'll tell you then. You'd have begged me. You'd have gotten down
on your knees and begged me. Sometime you will too. Wait and see.

LAURA: That's enough.

BEEBO: *(Pulls the bra that Laura has just put on, off of her.)* Laura hates me. Laura hates me.

LAURA: You're an animal.

BEEBO: Sure. Ask Jack. that's his favorite word. We're all animals.

LAURA: You're nothing but a dirty animal.

(She grabs a hairbrush and flings it at Beebo. Beebo grabs at her and embraces her.)

LAURA: Don't touch me.

BEEBO: You didn't mind last night. I touched you all over. Did I miss a spot?

LAURA: Let me go Beebo. I want to leave.

BEEBO: You're not going anywhere Bo-Peep.

(She begins to kiss her.)

LAURA: No. Beebo no.

BEEBO: I can't help myself anymore than you can. All right, go home to Marcie. Go home until you can't stand it. And when the pressure gets too great, come back down again. Come back to Beebo, your faithful safety valve.

LAURA: Beebo, I didn't come to you last night just because of Marcie.

BEEBO: No?

LAURA: No, I came, because . . .

BEEBO: You came, baby. That's enough. You came and I am not sorry and neither are you. The situation isn't perfect, but last night was perfect. *(Pulls the slip off Laura's shoulders.)* There's no hurry.

LAURA: Beebo, I've got to get up. I have to get to work.

BEEBO: To hell with work! This is love.

LAURA: Don't keep me Beebo. I need this job. I don't want to be late. I have to go home and change.

BEEBO: Call them and tell them you're sick.

LAURA: I can't.

BEEBO: Laura, you're not going to work.

LAURA: What makes you such an angel in bed and such a bitch out of it?

BEEBO: Want some coffee?

LAURA: I don't want another thing from you.

BEEBO: Not for another day or two.

LAURA: Beebo, I didn't mean to hurt you. I never made a secret of my feelings for Marcie.

BEEBO: Too many Marcies in your life, and you commit suicide. That's what it is to be gay, Laura. Sometimes all it takes is one. But you go and find out for yourself. I can't stop you. Jack can't stop you. Go play with your little Marcie. You'll find out soon enough she has claws. And teeth. And when you get to playing the wrong games, she'll use them. Go on baby. You've been warned. And then come back to stay. Or don't come back at all. I mean it Bo-Peep.

LAURA: There won't be a next time. Goodbye Beebo.

BEEBO: You'll be back little Bo-Peep.

CAGELOVE
Christopher Denham

Dramatic
Katie and Ellen, twenties

> *Katie and Ellen are sisters. Katie has just told Ellen that she has been raped by her ex-boyfriend.*

> *Early Thursday evening. Ellen is there with Katie.*

ELLEN: How do you feel?
   (Katie gives her a big thumbs-up.)
ELLEN: You need anything? Tylenol? *(Pause.)* Vitamins?
KATIE: Oh my God, stop.
ELLEN: Why can't I help you?
KATIE: Why can't you help me? Are you actually asking me that.
ELLEN: Of course I'm actually —
KATIE: *(Over her.)* You come in here, wearing that outfit like you're actually supposed to fool someone or —
ELLEN: What's wrong with my —
KATIE: *(Over her.)* That's a pantsuit! You're wearing a pantsuit!
ELLEN: I know a good psychologist
   (Katie grunts.)
ELLEN: No, he's good. I'm not telling you this because I'm worried. I'm telling you this because he's good. He works with artists, a lot, too.
KATIE: Because we're tormented? Because we can't get jobs?
ELLEN: Because you've been raped.
   (Katie stands.)
ELLEN: Please can you just — can you just hear me for a second?
ELLEN: Did um — can I ask how it happened?
KATIE: No.
ELLEN: I mean, not like details but just —
KATIE: No. I'll walk you out.

ELLEN: I mean, I know him, you know? He —

KATIE: You don't know him.

ELLEN: I don't know him? That's right, it wasn't me who bailed him out when he stole those acrylics from Ace Hardware for that like ten foot painting of your face. That —

KATIE: And what did he say? Did he ever tell you thanks? He said —

ELLEN: I know what he —

KATIE: *(Over her.)* He said to stay out of his life cause you quote "weren't made of anything real!"

ELLEN: How's the wedding stuff?

KATIE: We're good. *(Pause.)* Except for uh the caterers who — my friends are all vegans so the cake is gonna taste like goat shit and the tailors who — I went in the other day and found out you and all the bridesmaids' little outfits are all like Cindy Lauper rejects. And the jazz band that cancelled and now we have to hire a DJ who'll play M C Hammer all night!

ELLEN: I can go talk to the tailors if you want. There's a way to talk to these people.

KATIE: Nah.

ELLEN: Honey, look, I can do it! You want it a certain way, that's how you get it! It's just being firm with them.

KATIE: No, it just sucks. Mom should be here doing that. She calls me at the hospital saying she "hopes everything is all right". Not "can I come there and help" but — I mean — how can she not come?

ELLEN: I know.

Do you wanna sit?

KATIE: No.

ELLEN: Yes, you do.

(Ellen leads Katie to the bed.)

KATIE: You know — something happened to your kid — you go see your kid.

ELLEN: I'll call her.

KATIE: I don't want her here. She'd just be dour and use her unnecessary British accent. *(Pause.)* You know, when this whole thing goes through and me and Sam are — you know — it'll be sooo good to say I'm nothing like Mom. Bouncing around to whatever euro-trash passes as companionship in her circle. I swear, I'm not gonna be fifty years old, living in hotels, boasting to my Botox friends about whatever upper crust man I'm trying to, you know, take a bite out of. That WTO thing in London, Mom, not knowing who he was, actually tried to pick up Noam Chomsky. What the fuck is that? I am not going to be that lady!

ELLEN: Me neither.

KATIE: You won't be. I'm sure.

ELLEN: No, I will not.

KATIE: Don't get defensive.

ELLEN: I'm not.

KATIE: *(Pause.)* You're like pissed. Your face is all pissed.

ELLEN: Not really.

KATIE: Oh, I get it. Marriage stuff. That's what this is.

ELLEN: Marriage is great. Mars Jupiter compromising. Great.

KATIE: It's OK to be jealous.

ELLEN: What makes you think I'm jealous?

KATIE: 1986. Kenny Ames. The boy next door. You. Him. The tent made out of Care Bears. I mean, not like the hide of Care Bears . . . And you and Kenny were husband and wife. Ten years old. Playing house. But you took it so seriously, like how you were gonna afford that month's power bill and shit.

ELLEN: So?

KATIE: You were ten years old! That is so fucked up.

ELLEN: You liked him, too. *(Over her.)* Oh, yes you did. And he would always avoid you cause you were so young and you always wanted to like wrestle.

KATIE: He did not avoid me.

ELLEN: *(Over her.)* Yes, yes he did cause you always wanted to wrestle.

KATIE: Yeah, I was into wrestling back then.

ELLEN: Kenny Ames, my ten year old husband, avoided you, Kate. And you are still bitter.

KATIE: Kenny Ames, I'll say it again, did not avoid me. *(Pause.)* In fact, it was quite the opposite summer before high school when he popped me one underneath the deck.

ELLEN: Popped you one? Oh, that's classy.

KATIE: I'm just saying he didn't avoid me.

ELLEN: And I'm saying classy. *(Pause.)* Did you really have sex with him?

KATIE: Blame Kenny, man. All I did was lay there.

(Ellen stands, goes to her purse.)

ELLEN: I have Sam's cellphone number. Just tell him I'll call him later?

KATIE: What did you just say?

ELLEN: I said be nicer to me.

KATIE: How did you get his number?

ELLEN: He called me before. I just have to call him back.

(She starts to leave.)

KATIE: Wait. I'm sorry.

(Katie cuts off Ellen at the door.)

KATIE: I'm like kicking you out. We didn't even talk. I mean, not really. Not about . . . how school is. How's school?

ELLEN: Are you being nice?

(Katie sits Ellen down at the table.)

ELLEN: School is good. I mean, if you like ten hours of lab work where all you do is listen to children repeat nonsense syllables just so my professor really knows I really understand the "experimental" psychology of Hermann Ebbinghaus. I don't wanna bore you.

KATIE: You're not.

ELLEN: It's just science stuff.

KATIE: I know.

ELLEN: It's complicated.

KATIE: Well, contrary to public belief, I am not a monkey.

ELLEN: How are your pictures coming?

(Pause.)

ELLEN: I guess I'll go then. Paperwork awaits. Thanks for being nice to me.

KATIE: I need a favor.

ELLEN: *(Pause.)* . . . OK.

KATIE: I told Sam I went to see you last night.

ELLEN: But you didn't.

KATIE: Exactly.

ELLEN: OK. Well, where did you go? *(Pause.)* OK.

KATIE: You're not gonna um — you know —

ELLEN: Call Sam? Don't worry, I know I'm on Sam probation. *(She comes close to Katie.)* I'm just trying to help you, you know.

KATIE: OK.

ELLEN: You know you need it.

KATIE: OK.

(Ellen hugs Katie.)

KATIE: Please stay away.

(Blackout.)

CROOKED
Catherine Trieschmann

Dramatic
Laney and Maribel, teens

> *Laney has recently moved to a new town. She meets Maribel and the two become friends. Maribel is a serious Christian, whereas Laney has no faith. Laney has agreed to give Jesus a try if He gives her some sort of sign of his existence. Here, Maribel has taken Laney to her church to pray for a sign from Jesus.*

> *Laney and Maribel sit in the church choir loft. It is dark. Maribel hands a flashlight to Laney. They turn on the flashlights.*

LANEY: I like the sanctuary like this. Empty.

MARIBEL: You said you liked the service.

LANEY: I did. I just like it better like this. Quiet.

MARIBEL: You said you wanted to convert. If you convert, you have to go to service.

LANEY: I know.

MARIBEL: You could have converted during the service.

LANEY: I didn't want to convert during the service. I want to convert with you. Alone. There's nothing wrong with that, is there?

MARIBEL: No.

LANEY: I like your Mom.

MARIBEL: Why?

LANEY: She's quiet. My Mom's never quiet. I'm still not talking to her. She's so embarrassing. God . . .

MARIBEL: You can't do that.

LANEY: What?

MARIBEL: Take the Lord's name in vain like that. If you're going to convert, you have to stop doing that.

LANEY: OK.

MARIBEL: Are you ready?

LANEY: We should eat first. I brought some cake from the potluck.

MARIBEL: We can't eat in here.

LANEY: Come on, It's a special occasion. I'm gonna get saved, right?

MARIBEL: Yes.

> *(Laney hands Maribel a piece of cake. They eat.)*
>
> I told my parents we were playing flashlight tag with the youth
> group. The youth group always plays flashlight tag on Friday nights.

LANEY: Why couldn't you just say we'd be here?

MARIBEL: We're not supposed to be here.

LANEY: Why not? I'm converting, right? They want me to convert, don't
they?

MARIBEL: Well you're not supposed to sneak into the sanctuary to convert. You're supposed to convert during the service, walk to the
front of the church while everybody sings, "Just as I am."

LANEY: I like this way better.

MARIBEL: Me too. *(Pause.)* The adults, they all think flashlight tag is a
Godly kind of fun. But it's not. I got fingered playing flashlight tag.

LANEY: How'd that happen?

MARIBEL: The whole point of playing flashlight tag is so you can hang
out in the dark woods with boys. One night, I was wearing a skirt,
and Marcus Grayson told me to come hide with him in this dry
creek bed, and while we were crouching there, I felt his fingers all of
sudden walking up my leg. I didn't move. But they kept walking up
my thigh, until he fingered me.

LANEY: Did it hurt?

MARIBEL: No, it didn't hurt. It felt good. Kinda. I just wish he had kissed
me is all. I've never been kissed. Have you?

LANEY: Sure. I kissed a boy at my school in Wisconsin. Quentin
Compson. We kissed in the library after school. We frenched. And
then we got interrupted by Mr. Caruthers.

MARIBEL: Who's that?

LANEY: The librarian. He was cool though. We didn't get in trouble or
anything. Mr. Caruthers just sent us outside.

MARIBEL: Have you ever been fingered?

LANEY: No.

MARIBEL: Well, if you want to get fingered, we can go play flashlight tag. Marcus Grayson isn't here, but Henry Bowen is, and he tries to finger everyone. He'd try to finger you, even though you got, you know, a hump.

LANEY: It's not a hump. I think it's slutty to be fingered.

MARIBEL: It's not like having sex. You can be fingered and still be a virgin.

LANEY: It's still slutty. Especially if the person doesn't kiss you.

MARIBEL: The next time I tried to hide with Marcus I followed him through the woods, but he kept zigzagging back and forth through the trees. When I finally caught up with him and tried to hold his hand, he said, "get away from me, you big fat cow." I laid down on the ground in the woods and got stigmata.

LANEY: I don't really think you're slutty. Marcus Grayson is an asswad.

MARIBEL: *(Giggling.)* You can't say that here.

LANEY: What?

MARIBEL: You can't cuss.

LANEY: I didn't cuss. I just said asswad.

MARIBEL: You said it again.

LANEY: You mean asswad?

MARIBEL: *(Laughing even harder.)* Laney, I'm serious.

LANEY: Don't be such a tightass.

MARIBEL: Laney!

LANEY: Asswad, tight ass, asshole, asinine.

MARIBEL: Stop it!

LANEY: Asinine is not a cuss word.

MARIBEL: It's not funny.

LANEY: Then why are you laughing?

MARIBEL: Because you're not being serious.

LANEY: I'm as serious as a cereal box.

(The laughing subsides. They both calm down a little.)

MARIBEL: Are you ready now?

LANEY: I guess.

MARIBEL: You have to be sure. It doesn't count if you're not sure.

LANEY: I'm sure. What do I have to do?

MARIBEL: First you have to confess your sin.

LANEY: OK. I confess my sin.

MARIBEL: No, you have to be specific. List all your sins.

LANEY: Aloud?

MARIBEL: Yeah. It's the first step in getting saved.

LANEY: Give me an example.

MARIBEL: OK. Dear Jesus, please forgive me for allowing Marcus Grayson to finger me. Cause even though being fingered isn't as bad as having sex, it's still a sin.

LANEY: But I've never been fingered.

MARIBEL: Well, you just have to list your other sins.

LANEY: OK. Like what?

MARIBEL: Like drunkenness and sloth and greed. Holding other idols before God. Stealing. Murder. Cussing.

LANEY: Dear Jesus, please forgive me for saying ass.

(They both start giggling.)

MARIBEL: You're not supposed to laugh.

LANEY: I'm sorry. It's just funny. The word, ass.

MARIBEL: Do you want Jesus to come into your heart or not?

LANEY: I guess. What's it feel like? When Jesus comes into your heart?

MARIBEL: It feels . . . it feels like even if nobody ever speaks to you, or hears you, or even touches you ever again, it doesn't matter, because everything's OK. All the pain you feel, it just goes away and everything's OK. Someone sees me and hears me and knows everywhere that I hurt. And he just takes all that pain on himself, so I don't have to feel it anymore. So I'm whole. So I'm healed.

LANEY: I'd like that. To be healed.

MARIBEL: You want me to help you confess?

LANEY: OK.

MARIBEL: Close your eyes and repeat after me. Dear Jesus . . .

LANEY: Dear Jesus . . .

MARIBEL: Please forgive me for my sins.

LANEY: Please forgive me for my sins.

MARIBEL: For using your name in vain . . .

LANEY: For using your name in vain . . .

MARIBEL: And for ignoring you for fourteen years . . .

LANEY: And for ignoring you for fourteen years . . .

MARIBEL: For my lustful thoughts and hurtful deeds . . .

LANEY: For my lustful thoughts and hurtful deeds . . .

MARIBEL: I ask forgiveness.

LANEY: I ask forgiveness.

MARIBEL: You say that if we confess with our mouths that you are God and if we believe in our hearts that you were raised from the dead, then we will be saved. Elizabeth Lane Waters, do you confess?

LANEY: I confess.

MARIBEL: Do you believe?

LANEY: I believe.

MARIBEL: Now ask Jesus to come into your heart.

LANEY: Come into my heart Jesus!

(Pause.)

LANEY: Nothing. I feel nothing. It didn't work.

MARIBEL: You have to mean it.

LANEY: I meant it!

MARIBEL: You have to really mean it.

LANEY: I really meant it.

MARIBEL: If you really meant it, it would work.

CROOKED
Catherine Trieschmann

Dramatic
Laney and Maribel, teens

> *Laney has recently moved to a new town. She meets Maribel and the two become friends. Maribel is a serious Christian, whereas Laney has no faith. Laney has agreed to give Jesus a try if He gives her some sort of sign of his existence.*

> *Laney approaches Maribel sitting on the bleachers.*

LANEY: Hey.

MARIBEL: Hi.

LANEY: I tried calling you yesterday. Did you get my message?

MARIBEL: Uh huh.

LANEY: I thought you were going to take me to church.

MARIBEL: My Mom didn't feel like driving out to get you.

LANEY: Why didn't you call and tell me?

MARIBEL: I did. Your phone was busy.

LANEY: Maybe we were trying to call one another at the same time. You know, synchronized.

MARIBEL: I figured Elise could take you, if you really wanted to come.

LANEY: I did want to come.

MARIBEL: Why didn't you then?

LANEY: I wanted to go with you. Look, I'm sorry I lied about my Dad. You want my dessert?

MARIBEL: No. I'm full.

LANEY: Well, will you at least look at me?

(Maribel turns around.)

MARIBEL: Sometimes Satan tricks me.

LANEY: What?

MARIBEL: When I was little, I tried to baptize Gabriel in the bathtub. I wanted to make sure he was saved, even though he was just a baby, so I ran the water in the bathtub, got Gabriel out of his crib and baptized him. He almost drowned, but my Mom came in and pulled him out. Then she laid her hands on me and said, "Satan, I bind you from my daughter, Maribel. Satan, I cast thee out!"

LANEY: Why?

MARIBEL: Because Satan was tricking me. Made me think I wanted to baptize Gabriel, just so's he could drown.

LANEY: I don't believe in Satan.

MARIBEL: You're saved now. You have to believe in Satan.

LANEY: No. I just believe in Jesus.

MARIBEL: I think Satan still tricks me sometimes, confuses me into thinking something's good, when it's really bad.

LANEY: Like what?

MARIBEL: Like you. Converting you. I think I did it wrong.

LANEY: Why?

MARIBEL: Because you're acting funny.

LANEY: How so?

MARIBEL: Your story.

LANEY: You didn't like it?

MARIBEL: No.

LANEY: What didn't you like about it?

MARIBEL: You know.

LANEY: It's a made-up story. It doesn't mean anything. It's fiction. You know what fiction is, right?

MARIBEL: Yes.

LANEY: That's all it is. It doesn't have anything to do with my conversion.

MARIBEL: You didn't write like that before.

LANEY: I was just trying to write in a different genre. You know what a genre is, don't you?

MARIBEL: Uh huh.

LANEY: What? What is it?

MARIBEL: You know.

LANEY: Yes, I do. I was just trying to write something different. A romance. My earlier stuff was realism. I wanted to try a romance this time. I didn't mean to freak you out.

MARIBEL: I didn't freak out.

LANEY: You weren't supposed to take it so realistically. Romance is not realistic.

MARIBEL: Oh.

LANEY: That's OK. I forgive you. I know you don't know all that much about writing. Like you don't know about genres and metaphors and stuff cause you're in remedial classes, so it's understandable that you wouldn't get it.

MARIBEL: I got it.

LANEY: No, you didn't.

MARIBEL: I'm not stupid. I got it. The girl in the field with the silky black hair. That's my hair.

LANEY: So?

MARIBEL: So, that story was about me.

LANEY: It wasn't about you. It was inspired by you.

MARIBEL: I don't want to inspire your romance.

LANEY: You and Marcus Grayson.

MARIBEL: Marcus?

LANEY: Yeah. He was the narrator.

MARIBEL: The narrator?

LANEY: Yeah, you know, the person describing the girl in the field. It was inspired by you and Marcus. You know, the story of how he fingered you. But it's not the real story. It's romance.

MARIBEL: But you said "I".

LANEY: So?

MARIBEL: You said, I walk my fingers . . . you know.

LANEY: So?

MARIBEL: So, I is you.

LANEY: No, it's not. I is the narrator. I is a made-up person. In this case, I is a made-up person inspired by Marcus Grayson. I guess I could see how it might bother you. But nobody knows it was inspired by you and Marcus, and it's not like I can control what inspires me.

MARIBEL: That story was about me . . . and Marcus?

LANEY: Yeah. You know the thing that happened in the woods. But also, I saw him looking at you.

MARIBEL: You did?

LANEY: Yeah, he was looking at you, all admiringly. With longing in his eyes.

MARIBEL: He was?

LANEY: Yeah. I saw it.

MARIBEL: When?

LANEY: On Friday. After school, when we were waiting for the buses.

MARIBEL: He was looking at me?

LANEY: Yeah. With longing in his eyes. Like he was thinking about how you . . . felt. And that's what inspired me to write the story.

MARIBEL: Oh.

LANEY: I didn't mean for it to freak you out.

MARIBEL: It didn't freak me out.

LANEY: You were talking about Satan and drowning and stuff.

MARIBEL: It didn't freak me out.

LANEY: Talking about Satan is pretty freaky.

MARIBEL: You have to believe in Satan if you're going to believe in Jesus.

LANEY: How come?

MARIBEL: Because if it weren't for Satan, then Jesus wouldn't have had to die on the cross.

LANEY: I thought Jesus died for my sins, not for Satan.

MARIBEL: Satan is sin. Satan is original sin.

LANEY: So my sin comes from Satan. That's cool.

MARIBEL: Why?

LANEY: Cause that means Satan is responsible for my sins. Blame him.

MARIBEL: No, that's not how it works.

LANEY: Well then explain it to me, because your religion doesn't make any sense.

MARIBEL: It's your religion too.

LANEY: I don't believe in Satan.

MARIBEL: You have to believe in Satan, if you believe in Jesus.

LANEY: Why?

MARIBEL: It's hard to explain . . .

LANEY: How am I supposed to believe in something when you can't explain it clearly?

MARIBEL: Satan is original sin.

LANEY: You've already said that.

MARIBEL: Satan makes us do bad things, but you can't just blame him . . .

LANEY: That doesn't make sense!

MARIBEL: Satan is . . .

LANEY: I'm waiting . . .

MARIBEL: Satan is . . .

LANEY: Go on . . .

MARIBEL: . . . a metaphor

(This stumps Laney.)

LANEY: For what?

MARIBEL: For the harm we've done to God. For the harm we do each other.

HUNTER GATHERERS
Peter Sinn Nachtrieb

Seriocomic
Wendy and Pam

> *Wendy and her husband are dinner guests of Tom and Pam. It is not going well.*

> *Wendy enters holding a large Ziploc bag filled with too much ice than would be necessary for even the largest head.*

WENDY: The ice was frozen!

PAM: It's supposed to —

WENDY: Together. I had to bang the tray thing on the counter. Why can't they fix that?

PAM: Maybe it's too difficult a problem to solve.

WENDY: Where'd they go?

PAM: Tom's going to stitch him in the bathroom.

WENDY: Oh. Good. Good. I keep forgetting Tom has a skill.

PAM: I should learn how to stitch.

> *(Wendy clutches the ice. A pause.)*

WENDY: I am feeling really mortal right now.

PAM: I'm glad you're OK.

WENDY: But am I? Really?

PAM: Did you get cut?

WENDY: Not literally.

PAM: We have never had a pot fall down like that before.

WENDY: Like a guillotine! I felt the wind in my hair. Poor Anne Boleyn.

> *(Awkward pause.)*

PAM: I should check the Internet and see if there have been similar incidents with that rack.

WENDY: Oh we all have a pot with our name on it somewhere in the great abyss. Orbiting, menacing, making seemingly innocent stew . . .

Who knows when the pot will fall? Harder. Faster. Blam. The end. Dented. Crushed.

(Pause.)

God I want babies.

PAM: I want a better pot rack.

WENDY: I'm not joking.

PAM: Neither was I.

WENDY: It's what we're made for. We have had a special purpose ever since that sacred day. The day our reason for living became known. Remember that, Pam?

PAM: Our desert solos?

WENDY: No, silly. 7th Grade.

PAM: Our charm bracelet business?

WENDY: Our periods, Pam.

PAM: Oh. Oh.

WENDY: We bled! For the first time! Together!

PAM: Yes we did.

WENDY: Bloody and fresh. Just like —

PAM: I forgot about that.

WENDY: How could you forget our first? The tears. The wonder. The snow. We became women that night.

PAM: I don't remember it being a fun moment.

WENDY: It was cosmic! On bunk beds, no less. Your poor father. I think about that every time I go to Tahoe.

PAM: They sold that house.

WENDY: No-one can sell our memory. How long ago was your last?

PAM: Oh. Um, I don't know, maybe a little over —

PAM AND WENDY: Two weeks ago?!

(Wendy claps once.)

WENDY: Still riding the tandem cycle after all these years!
Sisterhood. Ding. The light is green in the circle of life.
Circle of life.

(Pause.)

PAM: I have nightmares about becoming a mother.

WENDY: They have epidurals.

PAM: After that. I worry about forgetting to put plastic in all the sockets.

Not knowing whether to put them to sleep on their stomach, or their back, which is it? Holding them the wrong way. Teaching them the wrong lesson.

WENDY: If only crack whores had your worries, Pam. Don't you hear nature's tock ticking? It's deafening. We're running out of time.

PAM: Not anymore. There are lots of ways to start a family these days. We can always adopt.

WENDY: What is the point of marrying a handsome perfect stallion of a man if you're just going to buy a kid later on?

PAM: Companionship? Love? Trust?

WENDY: I'm sure Richard wants to be a father.

PAM: We've really never discussed it.

WENDY: He may have an opinion.

PAM: He's never said.

WENDY: Have you ever asked?

PAM: Have you?

WENDY: Maybe you should ask him, Pam. Ask him what he thinks about his idling legacy.

PAM: Goodness, you're putting a lot of pressure on me.

WENDY: Tom's barren.

PAM: Oh.

WENDY: Every single sperm in his nuts is a retard.

PAM: I didn't know that.

WENDY: How's that for irony. You with the stallion and me stuck with the glue factory.

(Wendy stifles a tear.)

PAM: Wendy?

WENDY: *(Beginning to cry.)* Sorry. I'm sorry. It's only my future slipping away.

WENDY: I am a lonely field horse, Pam. Sadly nibbling on hay. Dreaming that one day I might meet a kind, generous mare who happens to be horse-married to a prime, hoofing thoroughbred. And perhaps that generous mare doesn't want to be a mother herself and wouldn't mind unlocking the stable door and taking a long long trot to the mall, looking the other way so all the field horse's dreams can come true.

(Pause.)

PAM: Yes.

WENDY: Someone who would understand.

PAM: Mmm.

WENDY: Someone with unconditional love.

PAM: Yes.

WENDY: Is there someone, out there in the world, who could be that good?

(Blackout.)

KILLERS AND OTHER FAMILY
Lucy Thurber

Dramatic
Elizabeth and Claire, twenties

Elizabeth and Claire are lovers. Danny is Elizabeth's brother.
Something happened to Elizabeth and Claire wants to know what
it was.

CLAIRE: O.K., what's going on? What's happening here? Elizabeth, why
are you yelling at everyone? Why are you yelling at me? And what
is the shit going on between you and this guy?

ELIZABETH: I'm sorry, I'm so sorry. I'm gonna make them leave I
promise. I will — You have to give me a chance. There's something
wrong with me. Can you see? I never did change. I just moved
pieces of me around. It all depends on what you present first and
how hard you believe in it.

CLAIRE: Elizabeth —

ELIZABETH: Danny likes to play games. Danny always hated that I went
to college. He just wanted me home. I liked college though, it was
my favorite time. Of course, I'm having trouble remembering right
now —

CLAIRE: Elizabeth, what are you talking about?

ELIZABETH: Oh, I'm sorry, I always talk to you in my head. I've been talking to you all day. I already explained everything but — now when
you're here I don't know how — He likes to be told stories. That's
how it always starts. When I was little they were only fairy tales
from school . . . Sometimes when I was little and he would sit me
on his lap, I'd pretend his face was mine. If you look at us the right
way we look just the same. Of course all I really wanted was for him
just to hold me. That's why I didn't mind when he started kissing
me, because I wanted to be held so badly.

CLAIRE: Baby . . . what — ? You're scaring me — I don't understand what you're talking about.

ELIZABETH: Did you want to read my new chapter? I'm almost done —

CLAIRE: Not right now sweetie . . .

ELIZABETH: But I'm almost done.

CLAIRE: I know.

ELIZABETH: Remember what I told you before?

CLAIRE: When?

ELIZABETH: Before when we were kissing.

CLAIRE: Baby we're always kissing —

ELIZABETH: That's right. I wrote the next chapter. I really did. I'm only one chapter away and if I could finish. If I could finish. If I could turn it in, I might . . .

CLAIRE: Elizabeth what happened here today? Why are you — ? I don't know what to do. Elizabeth you need to speak to me clearly so I can know what to do. Baby you know how sometimes when you're working on your dissertation and you get worked up cause you don't know how to say the things you want to say? You know how that happens?

ELIZABETH: Yes.

CLAIRE: And you get all excited and you freeze.

ELIZABETH: Yes.

CLAIRE: You freeze and you can't write. You can't think.

ELIZABETH: Yes.

CLAIRE: And your forehead gets all wrinkled up and you make that funny face.

ELIZABETH: *(Laughing.)* Yeah, I do, I do I make a funny face.

CLAIRE: And you and me take a walk around the block.

ELIZABETH: Walk . . . ?

CLAIRE: Yes. We walk. Why don't we go take a little walk?

ELIZABETH: I can't leave my manuscript here with them they'll break it.

CLAIRE: Why don't we take it with us. We'll just walk around the block. We'll get some air — *(Elizabeth starts to cry.)* Hey, hey, baby hey —

ELIZABETH: We have such a nice life don't we?

CLAIRE: Yes we do.

ELIZABETH: I love our life. I don't want to lose it.

CLAIRE: Why would you lose it?

ELIZABETH: Don't you see that they'll never let us go? He's killed somebody you know? That's why he's here. Beat some girl to death drunk
off his ass. That's why he's here.

CLAIRE: Are you serious?

ELIZABETH: I understand how it could happen. I mean, I could see
myself doing it if I were him. Because I've always loved him.

CLAIRE: You're not joking! We have to call the police. I'm calling the
police! Jesus we've just been sitting here this whole time — *(She
heads towards the phone.)*

ELIZABETH: *(Catching Claire's arm.)* He's my brother Claire, he's my
fucken brother —

CLAIRE: So?

MANNA
Cheri Magid

Dramatic
Madeleine, thirty-four; Bess, twenty-six

> *Madeleine and Bess are sisters. Bess, concerned about Madeleine's lack of a job, has come over to help her explore her options.*

> *Maddie and Bess entering Maddie's apartment, carrying Maddie's supplies, and unsold goods.*

MADELEINE: Oh my — did you see all those tents? There were like a hundred. And all the farmers and bakers from all over the place. Maybe I should hire him, you know, that kid, the one with the dreads, the one that was eating everything. I mean, it was really busy. Besides I'd like to see what other stuff people had, go talk to them, get a feel for the — do you think people are out there in the winter? I guess I need one of those heaters, or sell coffee. Or drink coffee. Oh my God they paid me. They gave me dollar bills and twenties and I needed to make change. I'm going to go count it.
(Madeleine begins counting.)
BESS: . . . where did you learn how to make all that Jewish stuff?
MADELEINE: $50, $70, $75 —
BESS: I mean, you told me about the challah. But that was only like three days ago. And God knows Mom never . . . did you take some kind of an intensive or — ?
MADELEINE: I have $300!
(She returns to counting.)
BESS: Yeah. So bake, you're going to bake . . . OK. Who do we know who. . . . Ravi's sister has that celebrity bakery downtown . . . maybe we could get you a job apprenticing or . . . Ravi says she's a psycho though. Course Ravi's a psycho so who really . . . you're not catering. They'll make you a waitress to like move up the ranks and then

you never know who you might be serving, it could be totally embarr . . . Jesus, what are the good jobs in the food industry? . . . I need paper do you have paper?

(Bess begins going through Madeleine's kitchen.)

MADELEINE: Hey. What are you doing?

BESS: Looking for paper. Listen I know you get all bent out of shape about this kind of thing but can I please hire you a cleaning woman? There's a lot of gunk forming around the edges of your cab—

MADELEINE: Can you not go through my stuff?

BESS: I'm just looking for some — oh I bet there's some in the trunk.

(Maddie continually tries to block her path.)

MADELEINE: No there's not — Bess. Just. We were just talking here. Can't we just sit and just have a good time and not think about anything right —

BESS: No. We are coming up with a list. Now.

(Maddie thrusts a phone book at her.)

MADELEINE: Here.

BESS: Why are you handing me a phone book?

MADELEINE: There's paper. There's that note section in the back.

(Beat. Bess takes the phone book.)

BESS: . . . OK. We are going to sit down and make a list of all of your options. Union Square, it's great, it's a great part-time, lunch-money type of gig. But you need to think about the big picture here. You've got your cost of living, and then if you do do this, there's your over-head — that's your man hours, equipment costs, transportation —

MADELEINE: Wait — I don't even know if I'm going to do this. I haven't made any decisions yet.

BESS: Well that's why we're going to give you options. Oooh. A live-in chef. To like a star or a CEO or something. You'd get a whole new living situation with maid service oh this is brilliant.

(Taking a bite of one of the pastries.)

Mmm. What'd you put in here?

(Maddie grabs it away from her.)

MADELEINE: No.

BESS: Maddie. Come on. I was eating that. I didn't even have breakfast.

(Maddie starts throwing the leftovers away. All of them.)

Wait. What are you doing?

(She gets up, goes over, tries to stop her.)

Stop. I was going to — these were going to be for the office. They were going to be samples —

(Maddie starts throwing the pots away and the knives.)

Stop it. Stop it. Don't do this. Please don't do this. Maddie I'm sorry I didn't mean to — whatever I said I take it back —

MADELEINE: *(Delivered to an unseen Mr. Iefshahr.)* You want me to choose? Well I choose to be left alone. Are you happy?

BESS: No I wasn't saying that was what you should — you're twisting everything around.

MADELEINE: So go away already! Leave me alone!

BESS: Stop it stop it stop it! Why do you always have to ruin everything! You do this. You you back out. You get all enthusiastic about whatever and then you break your ankle before your first audition or you lose your camera after someone paid you $500 to — God would it kill you to follow through? Would it kill you? Answer me!

MADELEINE: I . . . I

BESS: This is about me, isn't it? You're still punishing me. God is there nothing I can do to — I'm going to go.

MADELEINE: Bess. I'm not — it's not — listen. Listen. This really doesn't have anything to do with you. I prom –

BESS: Of course not. Why would it have anything to do with me?

MADELEINE: Will you — Listen. Listen to me. Just stop for a second, OK?

(Bess stops.)

Look. I don't know how to tell you . . . oh my . . . what I did to get the batter Bess. . . . I — look, if I keep doing this, something really bad is going to happen.

BESS: Maddie it's not . . . look. I know you're scared, OK? But whatever you did, you did it. It's inside of you, it's not going to go anywhere. I'll do whatever. Please. Let me help you. Let me — let me fix it. Please.

MADELEINE: . . . OK.

BESS: OK?

(Maddie nods almost imperceptibly.)

Oh my God yeah!

(Bess throws her arms around her.)

Oh this is going to be so great. OK. So I've already thought about the first thing we could do. Forget all the other stuff I was talking about. We'll keep it simple. My fund manager, Morris Schactor, he's having this — this thing, this get together no big deal —

(Maddie suddenly grabs Bess and hugs her to her tightly. We see her stricken face.)

Oh.

(Bess hugs her back awkwardly. Hold. Then Bess steps away.)

Um . . . anyway um — I overheard Morris saying how there were no good caterers anymore, and and I was thinking, with what you do this might be the perfect . . .

(Slow fade to black.)

(In the dark, a long long long pregnant pause. Then the sudden loud sound of a particularly foreboding doorbell. Madeleine and Bess appear in spot in the doorway of Morris and Aviva Schactor's Upper East Side brownstone. Madeleine is in the exact same spot and position as in the last scene, bug eyed. Bess is dressed up and clearly nervous.)

MADELEINE: . . . I really don't think this is a good idea.

BESS: You said that. Just remember to breathe.

MADELEINE: But I really think we should go. I think we should go right now. They're obviously not home anyway —

BESS: Oh they're home.

MADELEINE: Maybe they went away. Maybe they had an emergency. Maybe there was a big fire and they all had to evac —

BESS: Shhh. They're coming. It'll be fine.

MADELEINE: This is the last time I'm doing this. Do you hear me? The last time I ever —

MARIE ANTOINETTE: THE COLOR OF FLESH

Joel Gross

Dramatic
Marie Antoinette and Elisa, twenties

> *Elisa has been commissioned by the Queen of France to paint her por-*
> *trait and the two women have become close. The Queen has recently*
> *given birth to a son, but her heart belongs to an impoverished aristo-*
> *crat who has gone off to America to fight for its independence.*

> *An unseasonably warm day in October 1781. Marie Antoinette*
> *continues to scream, looking around vainly for help from someone,*
> *anyone on the otherwise empty stage. Finally her screams subside.*
> *She is exhausted. Elisa enters and goes to her at once. Elisa wipes*
> *the Queen's feverish brow, but the Queen shrugs her off, and strug-*
> *gles into a seated position.*

MARIE ANTOINETTE: My wrap. *(Elisa brings another blanket to the bed to*
wrap the Queen, but Marie Antoinette angrily pushes it aside.) My
wrap. *(Elisa is astonished to realize that the Queen wants a dressing*
gown, so that she may get out of bed.)

ELISA: You mustn't get out —

MARIE ANTOINETTE: *(With regal authority.)* Bring my wrap at once. *(Elisa*
brings her a dressing gown as the Queen laboriously swings her legs out
of bed. Hurriedly, Elisa drapes the Queen in the gown. Marie Antoinette
sits there for a moment, too exhausted to gather her thoughts coherently.
Hurt:) Why didn't you come?

ELISA: *(Gently reminding her.)* I am not allowed into the Queen's —

MARIE ANTOINETTE: *(Angry.)* Fifty of them, and not one a friend. How
could you leave me to them?

ELISA: Dear heart, only nobles of royal blood are allowed during the
delivery.

MARIE ANTOINETTE: Seven hours of hell. All around the bed on benches and chairs, fanning themselves calmly while I screamed! *(Wildly accusing.)* I needed you —

ELISA: I'm sorry.

MARIE ANTOINETTE: *(Remembering Elisa's words.)* He would leave me alone as soon as I am pregnant. Mother had sixteen children. Sixteen times she suffered this. Sixteen! *(Crazily explaining.)* No one will be satisfied with a girl. It's a girl!

ELISA: Toinette, dear heart —

MARIE ANTOINETTE: It must be a boy.

ELISA: *(Calmly and reasonably.)* Darling, listen. It is a boy.

MARIE ANTOINETTE: What boy?

ELISA: You have given birth to a boy. Your second child. *(Gently.)* Surely you remember?

MARIE ANTOINETTE: *(Slowly.)* Yes. Of course, I remember. A boy. They brought him to me.

ELISA: An heir to the throne of France.

MARIE ANTOINETTE: *(Slowly.)* And my daughter?

ELISA: Marie-Therese-Charlotte is already nearly three years old. *(Explaining.)* You are just tired. It is natural.

MARIE ANTOINETTE: Natural to forget to whom I have just given birth? I am a madwoman.

ELISA: No, dear heart.

MARIE ANTOINETTE: And all for what? It is too late for a son. The people will say that it is not the King's.

ELISA: No one will dare —

MARIE ANTOINETTE: Of course they'll dare. I haven't lived in France for eleven years and learned nothing. They will say what they like, if not to my face, then behind my back. If you listen carefully, you can hear the entire country whispering. Like crickets, like locusts beating their wings. Kiss me. *(Elisa kisses the Queen tenderly.)*

ELISA: Please, come back into the bed.

MARIE ANTOINETTE: Brush my hair.

ELISA: First get under the covers.

MARIE ANTOINETTE: No! Brush my hair. It's all knots. I need to sit up. Go ahead. Brush it. *(Elisa begins to brush the Queen's hair. Marie*

Antoinette begins to cry. Elisa puts down the brush and holds her as she sobs. Marie Antoinette suddenly breaks out of the embrace and stands. She is very shaky, and Elisa shadows her with concern.) They will never forgive poor Louis for marrying an Austrian. They hate me.

ELISA: You will exhaust yourself going on this way.

MARIE ANTOINETTE: I want to dress.

ELISA: You cannot.

MARIE ANTOINETTE: Don't tell me! Call Jeannette. I want to dress. I want to go. *(The Queen stalks clumsily downstage, where she stares into an unseen mirror.)* I am as fat as a butcher's wife.

ELISA: You are lovely.

MARIE ANTOINETTE: Bloated. Swollen. Why is Jeannette not here to dress me?

ELISA: Dear heart. *(Takes her hands.)* You are ice-cold.

MARIE ANTOINETTE: I have given Louis a son. Now I want to go out. To Paris. To enjoy elegant people, to gamble, to dance. Everything against which Count Alexis de Ligne cautioned me. *(She turns from the mirror, and takes a couple of clumsy dance steps before faltering. Elisa catches hold of her and guides her back to the bed. The Queen sits down heavily.)* He was to come back in "a few months." Four years! I suppose being a hero on horseback is just too much fun to give up. I suppose playing in the mud with George Washington is more important than anything —

ELISA: No one imagined the war would last so long. *(Elisa pours some tea from a silver service.)*

MARIE ANTOINETTE: I don't care when he comes back! Advising me not to go to masked balls! Where does he think we met in the first place?!

ELISA: *(Bringing the tea.)* That was seven years ago, my dear. Before the crop failures, the bankruptcies. More than ever, the people watch every move that you make. *(Encouraging her to drink.)* Please —

MARIE ANTOINETTE: Where do you think all this money is going? To his stupid little war! And for what? He's dead, of course, he's dead —

ELISA: You mustn't say that.

MARIE ANTOINETTE: If he is alive, he knows I had a child three years ago. He knows I was due to give birth again.

ELISA: How could he know this on an American battlefield? It might as well be the moon!

MARIE ANTOINETTE: Even on the moon they pay attention to the birth of kings. *(Despairing.)* I would have heard from him. He is dead.

ELISA: *(Insisting.)* I swear to you, if anything had happened to Alexis, I would know.

MARIE ANTOINETTE: How?

ELISA: I would feel it, Toinette. *(Tentatively explaining.)* I am sensitive to these things.

MARIE ANTOINETTE: *(Sarcastic.)* Of course. You are an artist, and close to every pagan god.

ELISA: He is not dead. He will be back. He will be back. *(Insisting.)* Say it.

MARIE ANTOINETTE: *(Repeating the incantation.)* He will be back. *(Pause.)* He will be back, only to find me a matronly, sluggish, corpulent thing. *(Suddenly.)* I even look fat in your portraits.

ELISA: You look perfectly wonderful in my portraits.

MARIE ANTOINETTE: But fatter! You cannot deny that you have painted —

ELISA: You are a woman, a queen, no longer a girl.

MARIE ANTOINETTE: Yes. But you needn't remind me of that in your paintings. I loved your early portraits. I was young, thin. Innocent. Even Mother — The only thing about me of which Mother approved was my image on canvas. *(The Queen gets under the covers, shivering as Elisa covers her. Suddenly the Queen grabs hold of Elisa with great force.)* I am so unhappy.

ELISA: You have a son.

MARIE ANTOINETTE: I hate him.

ELISA: Don't say —

MARIE ANTOINETTE: And my daughter!

ELISA: Please, dear heart.

MARIE ANTOINETTE: Little sniveling cowards. I hate them and I hate Louis. *(Explaining.)* He will want another and another. That is what women are for. You taught me that.

ELISA: No matter how gloomy the world may seem, I assure you —

MARIE ANTOINETTE: Assure me of what? The people hate me. The man I love will never come back to me. I have nothing. I wish I was dead!

ELISA: *(Pause.)* You are right, my darling. *(Explaining.)* You have given Louis a son. Naturally you want to go out.

MARIE ANTOINETTE: To Paris!

ELISA: Of course to Paris.

MARIE ANTOINETTE: Gambling, and dancing —

ELISA: Naturally. No one dances more beautifully.

MARIE ANTOINETTE: Why shouldn't I dance?

ELISA: You're entitled to some pleasure. When you are ready to leave your bed you will come with me. To the opera, to the great balls, everywhere there is amusement.

MARIE ANTOINETTE: *(Smiling.)* What of the people, the dangerous people watching my every move?

ELISA: Let them watch. You are the Queen and can do as you please!

MARIE ANTOINETTE: Go to my table. *(Pointing imperiously.)* Go! *(Elisa gets up and crosses to a table.)* I meant to do this last week. I was certain I would not live another day —

ELISA: *(Sharp.)* If you love me, you will once and for all stop talking about your living and dying —

MARIE ANTOINETTE: You have more superstitions than a fish-wife. *(Pointing.)* The box. Do you see the green leather box? Open it. *(Elisa opens the box and is taken aback by the sight of a beautiful emerald necklace.)*

ELISA: It's beautiful.

MARIE ANTOINETTE: Put it on. *(Elisa pulls the glittering chain of stones from the box, staring at them wonderingly, hesitating.)* Show a little respect for royalty. Do as you're told. Put it around your neck. *(Elisa turns to the unseen mirror and looks at her image as she clasps the precious necklace around her neck.)* Come to me, Elisa. Let me see. *(Elisa turns to her.)* Yes, it's as I thought. Emeralds suit you brilliantly. *(Explaining.)* A present. *(Not letting her protest.)* A present for you. My dearest friend. My companion in excess.

ELISA: I don't know what to say.

MARIE ANTOINETTE: "Thank you."

ELISA: "Thank you," Your Majesty. *(Embracing her.)* Thank you, dear heart.

MAURITIUS
Theresa Rebeck

Dramatic
Mary, about thirty; Jackie, mid-twenties

> *Jackie has inherited a stamp collection which, she has recently learned, may contain the world's rarest stamp, possibly worth millions. Mary, her older sister, believes the stamp collection is hers.*

MARY: Let's see what else do I know about Mauritius. They have beautiful white sand beaches. I dislike the beach, don't you? All that sand, the way it grinds on your teeth, I don't know why anyone enjoys the beach, really. Do you like the beach?

JACKIE: I've never been.

MARY: You've never been?

JACKIE: No, I've never been.

MARY: To the beach? Any beach?

JACKIE: No. I've never been to any beach.

MARY: You've never seen the ocean.

JACKIE: Oh god. You know —

MARY: I just find that —

JACKIE: I'm not —

MARY: What? Why can't I even comment?

JACKIE: Because there's nothing to comment on. I've just never seen it. I will see the ocean. I will, I'll see it, I'll see it some day. I'm young. I'm I'm *young.*

MARY: *(Smiling at her, lovely.)* Of course you are! Of course you are! We don't have to talk about it. Let's see, where were we?

JACKIE: The stamps?

MARY: Oh yes. They had this stamp, the Mauritians — Mauritians, that sounds like Martians, could that be right? Oh well, actually, it wouldn't have been the Mauritians, it would have been the British, they took it over back when they were you know, taking things over, and in 1847, they printed one of the first postage stamps on earth. The fifth country, I think. The head of the young Queen Victoria — oh, look at this! I remember this!

(She holds up an ugly broach.)

JACKIE: Take it. Take all of it.

MARY: I'm sure you want some of it.

JACKIE: It's not worth anything.

MARY: Maybe not to anyone else, but to us — oh, look at this!

JACKIE: *(Off the stamp book.)* So it's worth a lot of money then. This Mauritian stamp.

MARY: It's considered the crown jewel of philately. It's quite a spectacular error.

JACKIE: Error?

MARY: Well, that's what makes it so valuable, the errors are what make it — well, you don't know anything about stamps, do you?

JACKIE: So what's the "error?"

MARY: Alongside her face are the words "Post Office." The printer was supposed to print the words "Post Paid." Post *paid*. Of course once you know that it makes sense, why would you put "Post Office" on a stamp? I wonder that sometimes. What was going through that man's head. While he made the first postage stamp, and put the wrong words on it, out there in the middle of the Indian Ocean.

(She thinks about this, moved. Jackie thinks too, looking at the stamps.)

JACKIE: So how much, a thousand, a hundred thousand? How much are stamps worth?

MARY: I have no idea how much it's worth, it's beside the point. I couldn't possibly sell it. Oh! Oh. I'm sorry. But you do realize that these are my stamps. Don't you? *(Beat.)* He was my grandfather. He wasn't your grandfather. These are — my stamps. If you want the jewelry —

JACKIE: I don't want the jewelry. I already said I don't want the jewelry.

MARY: Well, but — these weren't *her* stamps. These were my grandfather's stamps, they're not part of the general, this isn't —

JACKIE: This isn't what? I mean, you weren't here —

MARY: That's not exactly —

JACKIE: Not exactly what, not exactly true? That you weren't here?

MARY: Not exactly relevant, I was going to say.

JACKIE: It was relevant to me. That's why I asked, so many times. You got my messages, right? We really needed you, I needed, you know —

MARY: Yes, yes yes but — I'm sorry but could we stay on the point please?

JACKIE: The point is —

MARY: Look, I don't want to, we're just having a conversation. You asked about the stamps.

JACKIE: Yes I did, that's right I did —

MARY: So we're having a conversation! There's no will and it would be terrible if we had to probate anything, that would take years, and involve all sorts of legal issues, so it's great that we can talk about what is yours, and what is mine. I'm really thrilled to have the stamps back. I I don't know how they ended up in mother's hands. Grandfather and I spent so much time with these stamps. Making catalogues, and lists. Corresponding with other dealers. Grandfather actually had an extended correspondence with FDR about the Two Penny Post Office, he wanted to buy it but grandfather would never let it go. You just wouldn't. Let it go. You wouldn't.

(Beat.)

JACKIE: Wow. An extended correspondence with FDR. That's incredible. How much did he offer?

MARY: I don't know that they ever got that far.

JACKIE: *(Beat.)* Maybe you could look through these boxes, I cleared out that closet upstairs. It doesn't look like anything to me but what do I know.

(There is a buzz at the door. Mary continues to page through the book of stamps while Jackie continues to work.)

MARY: Look, the inverted Jenny! This was one of my favorites. I used to pretend that grandfather and I were flying in the airplane, upside down!

JACKIE: Are you getting the door?

MARY: What?

JACKIE: The door, didn't you hear the door?

MARY: Oh, I thought you were getting it.

JACKIE: I'm working.

MARY: All you have to do is ask.

JACKIE: That's what I'm doing, I'm asking.

MARY: And I'm getting it!

(She smiles and goes to answer the door. After she is gone, Jackie is alone in the room for a moment.)

JACKIE: *(To herself)* I hate her. I hate her so much. Oh god, I hate her.

MOMBO
Alan Gelb

Comic
Marsha and Dee, late twenties

> *Marsha and Dee are two mothers watching their sons' soccer game from the sidelines.*

> *Two mothers, Marsha and Dee, on the sidelines of a soccer game. They are dressed in super-bulky Patriots outerwear, with wool caps, mufflers, and mittens. Best played with broad Boston accents.*

MARSHA: *(Yelling.)* Way to go, Trevor! Way to be! On him! Yeah!

DEE: Move in, T.J.! Hustle! Hustle! Clear it!

MARSHA: *(Shaking her head.)* Oh, man. he got smoked.

DEE: It's that Panamanian kid. He's greased lightning.

MARSHA: Is it wicked cold out here today or what?

DEE: Goddamn April. Some joke.

MARSHA: Go, Trevor, go! Send it down! Ackland's open! Oh! Bad luck ! *(To Dee.)* He shoulda had that one.

DEE: Hey. It happens. No biggie. Just so long as he don't beat up on himself later.

MARSHA: Not as much as I'll beat up on him.

DEE: *(Guffawing.)* Oh, you're some kidder, Marsh.

MARSHA: Who's kidding?

DEE: Stop! You're killing me!

MARSHA: No, seriously — Trevor can be real hard on himself. And he hasn't been happy with his play lately.

DEE: Oh, come on, Marsh. Give me a break. The kid's awesome.

MARSHA: Yeah, you think so and I think so, but that don't mean Trevor thinks so. Come on, Madison! Come on, team! Mark up! Hey! Ref! That's a push! *(To Dee.)* Did you see that push?

DEE: That's why I hate Bonaventure. They play a mean, dirty game. I don't know why it's got to be like that.

MARSHA: I'm with you, Dee. Sometimes I feel like . . . I don't know . . . like the . . . *joy's* just gone out of the thing.

DEE: *(Tsks.)* Tell me about it.

MARSHA: It's just not right. It's got to be about more than just winning. There's got to be . . . Trevor! Move, will you? Damn, he's slow today. I don't know. Some days it's like his heart's just not in it. You know what I mean?

DEE: T.J. too. Some days he just kind of . . . *hangs* there.

MARSHA: Oh, come on, Dee. Teej is such a solid player. You know what our defensive line would look like without him? He's the heart and soul of this team —

DEE: Oh, please. If T.J. is the heart and soul of this team, then we're in deep doo-doo.

MARSHA: Will you stop? T.J. is Mr. Reliable. I mean, just look around. Nick M.'s on walkabout half the time. Chase Delaney's had so many injuries, I don't know what's holding him together. But Teej is our go-to man. The steady rudder of the ship —

DEE: Come on, Marsh. You're making me seasick. Nice touch, Trev! Stay with it! Good job!

MARSHA: You know, Dee, there's something I always wanted to tell you.

DEE: Uh-oh.

MARSHA: No, seriously — the way you cheer on all the kids, not just your own — that's really special. That's where T.J. gets his sports-manship. From you, Dee. I'm not kidding.

DEE: Yeah, well, you can be damn sure he don't get it from his goddamn father. That bum. Him and his mother, may she rest in peace . . .

MARSHA: She ain't dead, Dee.

DEE: Yeah, well, we can dream, can't we?

MARSHA: What's it now?

DEE: The usual bullshit. Edwin wants Teej to do Easter down in Delaware with the old bag. Put it wide, Teej! Get it off your foot!

MARSHA: Hey. At least Edwin *wants* his kid for Easter. Trevor hasn't seen Merle since I don't know when. Don't it drive you crazy? I mean, here we are, freezing our buns off out here, doing everything we can for these boys.

DEE: 'Cause that what mothers do.

MARSHA: You said it. Mother's work is never done. Trevor! Don't just stand there! Move it, will you!

DEE: I don't know what it is with these men.

MARSHA: It's their mothers, that's what. I mean, what kind of woman names her son "Merle"? But that's a whole other story. I'm not even going there. Hey! Ref! Did you see that? *(To Dee.)* Did you see that Panamanian kid? Did you see the shove? Ref! Open your goddamn eyes, will you?

DEE: That's why I hate Bonaventure.

MARSHA: Get an eye exam, Ref! I'm not kidding! *(Hugging herself and reaching for her thermos.)* Is it wicked cold out here or what! I swear, something's wrong with the universe it should be this cold. *(Offering the thermos.)* Want a hit?

DEE: Nah. Thanks anyway. Ever since they got rid of the Port-o-San, I limit my fluid intake at these things.

MARSHA: Yeah. Tell me about it.

DEE: I got it down to a fine science. Stop at the Dunkin' Donuts before the game, pee, grab a Munchkin, and hope for the best.

MARSHA: You'd think, for our tax dollars, they could get a goddamn Port-o-San out here. Come on, Trevor! Use your . . . oh, my God! It's a breakaway!

DEE: What?

MARSHA: Trevor! Get him! Get the Panamanian kid! Stop him! Stop him!

DEE: Stop him, Teej! Oh, my God! He got past Teej! *(An awful suspended moment of disbelief. Then the goal! Anguished head pounding and breast-beating follow.)*

MARSHA: Holy magoley. Did you see the way that kid found the corner?

DEE: There was no stopping him.

MARSHA: Where was our team? Sleepwalking!

DEE: It's OK, Marsh. There's time, there's time. *(Yelling to the team)* There's time, boys! There's time! You can do it, Madison! *(A depressed silence.)* It's those breakaways. You can't do anything about a breakaway.

MARSHA: *(Bitterly.)* Yeah. Whatever.

DEE: So what? It's T.J.'s fault?

MARSHA: Who said it was anyone's fault? Did you hear me say it was anyone's fault? *(A bristling silence.)*

DEE: It's only a game.

MARSHA: Yeah. Right. To you it's only a game and to me it's only a game. But Trevor takes it very seriously.

DEE: Oh, and T.J. doesn't?

MARSHA: I didn't say that. Did you hear me say that? Look, let's not go all negative here, OK? I don't want to send bad vibes down to the boys. *(Clapping her hands.)* Come on, Madison! You can do it! Let's go! Beat those Bonaventure . . . oh, shit! Here they come again! Stop him! Stop him!

DEE: Go, Teej! That's it! You got him! *(Seeing something, horrorstruck.)* Whoa! Ref! He's down! *(At the top of her lungs.)* Man down!

MARSHA: *(Shocked.)* Jeez. Teej. That kid went over him like a Mack truck.

DEE: Oh, my God. He's hurt. I better go see. *(Marsha puts out a hand to stop her.)*

MARSHA: What are you, crazy? He'll hand you your head. Just stay here. Let Coach handle it.

DEE: Coach? He couldn't find his way out of a paper bag, that moron. I gotta go see —

MARSHA: Dee, I'm telling you —

DEE: But what if he's really hurt?

MARSHA: He's not. OK? Look — he's up on his feet. *(Clapping.)* Big hand. Way to be, T.J.!

DEE: *(Worried.)* Is he walking funny?

MARSHA: *(Peering.)* Nah. No more than usual. C'mon, Madison! One minute! Make it happen! You can do it, Madison! Go! Go! *(Turning to Dee.)* I don't hear you.

DEE: Marsh, my kid just got hurt!

MARSHA: Oh, come on, will you? Look! Trevor's got it! Take it down, Trev! That's a boy! Oh, my God, does that kid have footwork or what? *(Dee gives Marsha a hateful look.)* Beautiful, Trev! Beautiful! Look at him go! Shoot, Trevor! Shoot! Shoot! *(And then horror.)* Oh!

DEE: *(With a spiteful grin.)* He got smoked.

MARSHA: That goddamn Panamanian kid!

DEE: *(Shaking her head.)* Greased lightning. *(From offstage comes the countdown.)*

[OFFSTAGE: Ten, nine, eight . . .]

MARSHA: *(Screaming wildly.)* Make it happen, Madison! Make it happen!

[OFFSTAGE: . . . seven, six . . .]

DEE: Marsh, get real. We don't even have the goddamn ball.

MARSHA: Go! Go! It's not over till —

[OFFSTAGE: . . . Five, four . . .]

DEE: — it's over.

[OFFSTAGE: . . . Three, two, one . . .]

> *(The horn blows. Marsha stands there, poised in the exquisite agony of the moment, and then sags.)*

DEE: You OK?

MARSHA: *(In a small lost voice.)* They were so close.

DEE: It's not the end of the world.

MARSHA: Yeah. Whatever. *(A profound silence.)*

DEE: You taking Trevor to Donny Molloy's party?

MARSHA: I don't know. I don't know if he'll even want to go now.

DEE: Are you kidding, Marsh? You ever meet a five-year-old kid who'd turn down a paintball party? Oh, God. T.J.'s crying. I'm coming, Teej! Mommy's coming! *(Dee rushes offstage, leaving Marsha by herself.)*

MARSHA: *(Under her breath.)* Goddamn Bonaventure. *(She gathers her things.)*

RUNES
Don Nigro

Dramatic
Vonnie, sixteen; Nancy, eighteen

> *It's early in the year 1898 in Armitage, a small town in east Ohio. Vonnie and her half-sister Nancy are upstairs folding laundry in a bedroom above Love's General Store, which is run by Arthur Wolf, who is Vonnie's father and Nancy's stepfather. Their mother, Evangeline, has told them that Nancy was the child of a young Bible salesman who was killed on the railroad tracks before they could marry, but in fact she's the product of a late night assault in the back room of the store by an unknown person. But Nancy has grown up adoring her stepfather Arthur, despite his cranky disposition. His wife and actual children, Vonnie and her brother Jonas, have never been able to warm up to him. And now that Evangeline has disappeared, Vonnie has begun to suspect that her father might have killed her mother, believing that Evangeline would never just run off and abandon them. Vonnie is a real beauty, a talented actress who's just played Juliet in a town theatrical production, and her teachers say she's a brilliant student. But she's also a troubled girl with a sharp tongue. Arthur says that Nancy, on the other hand, is what he would call, half in jest, simple-minded, but that's not really the case. Nancy is not as smart as her sister, but neither is anybody else, and she's a sweet girl with a reservoir of strength who can sometimes see things her brother and sister can't. Vonnie loves her sister and is increasingly afraid their now heavily drinking father might do Nancy some harm.*

> *Vonnie in the bedroom, watching Nancy fold laundry.*

VONNIE: Why do you do that?
NANCY: I fold laundry because you don't. It's all right. I don't mind.

VONNIE: Why do you wait on Papa hand and foot like you do? You act like you're his servant or something. You do everything he wants. You treat him like he was the Lord God Almighty.

NANCY: You like to read. I like to take care of Papa. What do you want me to do? Kick him down the steps?

VONNIE: That's be a good start, yes, but I'd be thrilled if you'd just stand up to him once in a while. He's not even your father.

NANCY: I know he's not my father. You don't have to remind me that he's your father and not mine.

VONNIE: I didn't mean it that way. I just mean I don't think it's right, the way he treats you.

NANCY: He's good to me.

VONNIE: He's not good to you. He treats you like you're his personal slave. It's not right.

NANCY: Why do you care how he treats me?

VONNIE: Because you're my sister.

NANCY: I'm your half sister.

VONNIE: Well, tell him to go to hell half the time and I'll be happy.

NANCY: *(Smiling at her.)* You're crazy, Vonnie.

VONNIE: So I've been told.

NANCY: I don't mean that as a criticism.

VONNIE: I don't take it as one. I consider it a badge of honor.

NANCY: I just mean that things go on in your head that don't go on in anybody else's, and sometimes those things get out, and you say things and nobody knows what you're talking about, or things you don't mean, that can hurt people. If you'd just try and be a little nicer to Papa he might be nicer to you. If you just love a person enough, sooner or later they've got to love you back.

VONNIE: No they don't. That's the stupidest thing I've ever heard. What kind of a world do you think we're living in, anyway? It doesn't work like that.

NANCY: You have your theory. I have mine. Neither one of us has been alive long enough to prove the other one's wrong.

VONNIE: I know you're wrong. Look at the way he treats you.

NANCY: He can't help it. He doesn't mean it. I'll win him over.

VONNIE: You've had your whole life to win him over. How long is it going to take?

NANCY: You don't want me to win him over.

VONNIE: I don't want you to keep getting hurt.

NANCY: But that's what love is. Getting hurt over and over again, for the person you love.

VONNIE: No it's not. That's not what love is.

NANCY: Then what is it?

VONNIE: I don't know what it is, but it's not that. That's just some kind of a sickness.

NANCY: I don't understand how you could be such a great Juliet and think like that.

VONNIE: That was a play. This is life.

NANCY: Do you know what your problem is, Vonnie? You're too smart to be happy.

VONNIE: I just hate seeing you run around doing everything for him. I'm against it. It's not good for you. It's not good for anybody.

NANCY: He's lost, since Mama ran away. He misses her real bad.

VONNIE: He doesn't miss her.

NANCY: He does, Vonnie. He's very lonely.

VONNIE: He's not lonely. He's happy she's gone.

NANCY: You don't understand him at all. He can't sleep. He walks around the house at night, talking to her. He goes downstairs to the store and paces back and forth and drinks and talks to her in the dark.

VONNIE: What does he say?

NANCY: He misses her.

VONNIE: He says that?

NANCY: He says a lot of things. Some of it I don't understand.

VONNIE: How do you know what he says when he's down there walking around at night?

NANCY: Sometimes I hear him. When I can't sleep.

VONNIE: Nancy, you don't go down there with him when he's like that, do you?

NANCY: He needs somebody.

VONNIE: You should stay away from him when he's like that.

NANCY: What do you think he's going to do? He'd never hurt me. He'd never hurt anybody. He's all bark and no bite. Haven't you figured that out yet? He doesn't mean half the things he says.

VONNIE: Nancy, just because you want to believe something doesn't make it true.

NANCY: It doesn't make it a lie, either.

VONNIE: Everything is a lie.

NANCY: Is that what you really believe? That nothing is true?

VONNIE: Something might be true, somewhere, maybe. But whenever you think you've found a piece of it, it always turns out to be a lie. Believing something always makes it a lie.

NANCY: That doesn't make any sense.

VONNIE: This is true. Which of course means it's a lie.

NANCY: Maybe you really are crazy.

VONNIE: Just promise me you won't go down there when he gets like that, OK?

NANCY: Somebody's got to.

VONNIE: Then I will. You just go back to sleep.

NANCY: Why you and not me?

VONNIE: Because I can protect myself. You can't.

NANCY: I don't need to protect myself.

VONNIE: Just do what I say. Can't you just do what I say?

NANCY: I'm the big sister. You shouldn't be telling me that. I should be telling you that. And you don't like me trying to take care of Papa, but, Vonnie, you try to take care of everybody.

VONNIE: No I don't.

NANCY: You do. You always have. You just do it in a different way. You were always sticking up for Mama and me and Jonas when we were kids. You'd go after people twice your size if they just looked crooked at us. You took the blame for things we did. You stood up to our teachers when everybody else was scared to. And you got away with a lot of things just because you're so smart and so beautiful. Well, that's fine for you, but I want to take care of people my way. I don't want to fight anybody. He just needs to be loved, Vonnie. He just needs somebody to love him. And that's something I know how to do. So just don't worry about me, all right?

VONNIE: You just be careful, OK? Because if that man ever hurts you —
NANCY: He's not going to hurt me.
VONNIE: If he ever does, I'll kill him.
NANCY: Vonnie, Papa's no danger to anybody but himself. And neither are you. You're very smart, and very brave, and you have a big heart, and you stand up to people, and that's a good thing, I admire that, I really do, but you know you would never really hurt anybody.
VONNIE: I could. And I will.

(Vonnie and Nancy look at each other as lights fade on them.)

SCHOOL OF THE AMERICAS

José Rivera

Dramatic
Julia, twenties; Lucila, teens

> *Julia and Lucila are sisters, living in a Bolivian village. There is*
> *fighting in the streets between the Bolivian army and guerillas led*
> *by Che Guevara, and they are staying inside to keep safe.*

> *Lucila goes to the window, looks out.*

LUCILA: You think they're gonna do that all night?

JULIA: Just what we need. Drunken soldiers acting like fools — on a
school night.

LUCILA: Rosa Anna says there's a *general* out there. Little stars on his
chest and his own helicopter! . . .
(Julia goes to the window, shouts.)

JULIA: You guys stop that! I'm telling you! Don't make me go out there!

LUCILA: Rosa Anna also told me there are *yanqui* soldiers out there, too.
The ones giving the orders are *yanquis*. And when they're done tor-
turing him here, they're going to take the Commandante to
Washington, D.C. for more torture.

JULIA: We will now put a moratorium on the foolish gossip of Rosa
Anna!

LUCILA: "Moratorium?" Wait, let me grab my dictionary, Miss Moratorium!

JULIA: There will be no torture in La Higuera! They wouldn't dare!

LUCILA: What's wrong with you? You don't realize a lot of important
work is taking place only a few feet from this house. Instead of
being honored, you're *agitated*. All day — a bad mood!

JULIA: When generals and helicopters land in your back yard, Lu, it's
time to get a little agitated.

LUCILA: But the men they captured are *terrorists*, Julia. Foreign guerillas.

JULIA: I heard the radio. I know what Barrientos wants us to think.

LUCILA: Everyone knows the guerillas have done nothing but murder peasants, steal chickens, and rape women —

JULIA: I never heard they rape women.

LUCILA: Rosa Anna heard it.

JULIA: Rosa Anna is an ignorant, old gossip who loves to make things up.

LUCILA: Why are you defending them? They're *atheists*. They worship money!

JULIA: Such ignorance! Communists *don't* worship money. It's why the *yanquis* hate them so much!

LUCILA: When men are *atheists* there's nothing they won't do. Men tell the truth *only* when they think God is listening. God, who knows *everything* . . .

(Julia knows this spiel by heart.)

JULIA: Don't try to out-God me. I know my God.

LUCILA: . . . checking the words men say against the knowledge He has of the Universe. Men don't steal when they know God's watching. They don't blaspheme, cheat on their wives, invade other countries, or rape little girls!

JULIA: Now the guerillas are raping little girls. What's next? Crucifying their grannies?

LUCILA: Look, I know I'm nothing but an ignorant, old fool, not a smart-ass like you and Papi —

JULIA: "Fool" is your word.

LUCILA: But I have two things better than education: faith and instinct. And my instincts are *loud* — warning me to be *careful*. To let our leaders do what they think is best and not let our big mouth get us in trouble.

JULIA: I will say whatever I want, whenever I want, to whoever I want. Little stars or no little stars.

LUCILA: You forget these guerillas are dirty, godless foreigners, girl, coming here uninvited to spill blood and take your land.

JULIA: So unlike the North Americans — who are good and wise and actually *belong* in Bolivia!

LUCILA: North Americans believe in God.

JULIA: You never met a North American in your life!

LUCILA: All I can say is when you come across these North Americans — and I know you will, 'cause you never listen to me — you are polite, civil, and you make them know we are people of great pride and greater respect.

JULIA: I know how to act in front of strangers.

LUCILA: These are not just strangers. They're strangers with very big guns.

JULIA: And you wonder why I'm in a bad mood.

(Beat.)

LUCILA: I know why you're in a bad mood. You saw him.

And by just looking at his face, you think — no, you *know* — he's a good man with a good cause and everything we hear on the radio from our side is a lie. Dear Lord, how did I end up living with such a romantic?

JULIA: I saw nothing romantic about the man they dragged into La Higuera like a dog.

LUCILA: That's not what Rosa Anna said. He's the most beautiful man she's ever seen.

JULIA: He looked like hell. Not like the pictures. More like one of those souls who lose their minds and wander the mountains like an animal.

LUCILA: Like Uncle Joaquin! I still cry!

JULIA: *Worse.* Uncle Joaquin really *did* lose his mind. He didn't understand there's indignity in sleeping in ditches, peeing in his clothes, walking on all fours, competing with the dogs for food. His body was in hell but in his mind he was a little boy, on his mother's lap, drinking her sweet milk and feasting on her love. No. The man they captured today wasn't lucky enough to lose his mind.

LUCILA: Maybe God wants that Communist to learn something.

JULIA: So the ropes tying his hands are meant to teach him a lesson? Wow! Maybe I'll try that with my kids. Point rifles at them, humiliate them . . . maybe my kids'll learn so much, they'll be as smart as the geniuses of North America!

LUCILA: Sarcasm is an ugly trait in a woman.

JULIA: Must be why I have so many suitors.

Lu, he looked so scared. He kept looking into the crowd for someone to help him. At one point he looked right at me. I swear, my heart jumped! I thought: this man had *everything* once, now he has nothing. What's it like to fall so far? Then the soldiers pushed us away from him.

Rosa Anna says they're keeping him in the school.

LUCILA: I thought we were putting a "moratorium" on —

JULIA: If that's true — first thing tomorrow — I'm going to the school to talk to him.

LUCILA: Wait; wait a *minute* —

JULIA: When Papi was alive if anything important happened in town, it fell on his shoulders. Since he's not here, it falls on me.

LUCILA: But he's a prisoner of the military!

JULIA: In *my* school! Every person who walks into that ugly, old building is my responsibility.

LUCILA: No, Julia. *No.* You are to stay *away.* Do not get mixed up in things you have no —

(Lucila stops, looks at Julia — and laughs long and loud.)

JULIA: Now what's wrong with you?

LUCILA: You really think you're gonna find a husband in that school?

JULIA: I swear, words fall out of your mouth and I —

LUCILA: Lonely Julia! No one in La Higuera's good enough for a snob like you. Now *here's* a man to make a girl proud! Famous, handsome and *muy macho!*

JULIA: I don't fool myself like that, shut up.

LUCILA: A sister knows her sister's heart!

JULIA: I know I'll never have kids of my own except a dozen boys and girls who go to that school. I'm resigned to it.

I want to know why he came to this country. What he thought he was going to accomplish. What he thinks of our people.

LUCILA: Uh-huh. And you won't be wearing your best dress, either. Dear Lord, how did I end up living with such a rebel?

JULIA: I thought you said I was a romantic.

LUCILA: The worst kind: a rebellious romantic. Dying to fuck everything up —

(Julia laughs, crosses herself.)

JULIA: Sis, your language!

LUCILA: You get in trouble with those soldiers, you're gonna hear worse. Life isn't hard enough? You're one of the few women with *a job*. Someone people look up to 'cause God gave you brains and dropped some fire in your heart. We have a decent home and don't you get it? — one wrong word with the North Americans and it could all go away, blown apart like something they hit with a bomb.

JULIA: Good thing they believe in God, huh?

LUCILA: You go to jail, what's gonna happen to me? Who's gonna take care of me? That awful, stupid Rosa Anna?

JULIA: I'm not going to jail. I'm going to work. I work in that school. If there's someone in there, I'm going to talk to him. Because that's what I do. I don't plant fields, herd cattle, or make babies. I talk to people.

LUCILA: Yes, you do. God help us all.

RIGHTS AND PERMISSIONS

Please note:
Performance rights holder is also the source for the complete text.

AMERICAN GIRLS. © 2008 by Hilary Bettis. Reprinted by permission of the author. For performance rights, contact Hilary Bettis (hbettis5@aol.com).
AREA OF RESCUE. © 2007 by Laura Eason. Reprinted by permission of Morgan Jenness, Abrams Artists Agency. For performance rights, contact Broadway Play Publishing, 56 E. 81st St., New York, NY 10021 (www.broadwayplaypubl.com).
ALL EYES AND EARS. © 2008 by Rogelio Martinez. Reprinted by permission of the author. For performance rights, contact Broadway Play Publishing, 56 E. 81st St., New York, NY 10021 (www.broadwayplaypubl.com).
THE BEEBO BRINKER CHRONICLES. © 2008 by Kate Moira Ryan and Linda S. Chapman. Reprinted by permission of Mary Harden, Harden-Curtis Assoc. For performance rights, contact Mary Harden (maryharden@hardencurtis.com).
CAGELOVE. © 2007 by Christopher Denham. Reprinted by permission of Carl Mulert, The Gersh Agency. For performance rights, contact Broadway Play Publishing, 56 E. 81st St., New York, NY 10021 (www.broadwayplaypubl.com).
CHERRY DOCS. © 2008 by David Gow. Reprinted by permission of J. Gordon Shillingford, Scirocco Press. For performance rights, contact J. Gordon Shillingford (durians@interlog.net).
CHICKEN. © 2005 by Mike Batistick. Reprinted by permission of Peter Hagan, The Gersh Agency. For performance rights, contact Dramatists Play Service, 440 Park Ave. S., New York, NY 10016 (www.dramatists.com).
CROOKED (2). © 2006 by Catherine Trieschmann. Reprinted by permission of Elsa Neuwald, William Morris Agency LLC. For performance rights, contact Elsa Neuwald (eneuwald@wma.com).
DEATHBED. © 2008 by Mark Schultz. Reprinted by permission of Olivier Sultan, Creative Artists Agency. For performance rights, contact Dramatists Play Service, 440 Park Ave. S., New York, NY 10016 (www.dramatists.com).
THE DIRTY TALK. © 2008 by Michael Puzzo. Reprinted by permission of Seth Glewen, The Gersh Agency. For performance rights, contact Dramatists Play Service, 440 Park Ave. S., New York, NY 10016 (www.dramatists.com).
THE DRUNKEN CITY. © 2008 by Adam Bock. Reprinted by permission of Val Day, William Morris Agency LLC. For performance rights, contact Samuel French, Inc., 45 W. 25th St., New York, NY 10010 (www.samuelfrench.com).
EARTHQUAKE CHICA. © 2004 by Anne García-Romero. Reprinted by permission of Susan Gurman, Susan Gurman Agency. For performance rights, contact Broadway Play Publishing, 56 E. 81st St., New York, NY 10021 (www.broadwayplaypubl.com).
ELECTION DAY. © 2008 by Josh Tobiessen. Reprinted by permission of Beth Blickers, Abrams Artists Agency. For performance rights, contact Samuel French, Inc., 45 W. 25th St., New York, NY 10010 (www.samuelfrench.com). The entire text has been published by Smith and Kraus, Inc. in *New Playwrights: The Best Plays of 2008.*
END DAYS. © 2007 by Deborah Zoe Laufer. Reprinted by permission of Derek Zasky, William Morris Agency LLC. For performance rights, contact Derek Zasky (dwz@wma.com).
EXTREMELY. © 2007 by Rolin Jones. Reprinted by permission of Chris Till, Creative Artists Agency. For performance rights, contact Broadway Play Publishing, 56 E. 81st St., New York, NY 10021 (www.broadwayplaypubl.com).
THE FARNSWORTH INVENTION. © 2008 by Aaron Sorkin. Reprinted by permission of Jack Tantleff, Paradigm Agency. For performance rights, contact Samuel French, Inc., 45 W. 25th St., New York, NY 10010 (www.samuelfrench.com).
GOD'S EAR. © 2008 by Jenny Schwartz. Reprinted by permission of Mark Christian Subias Agency. For performance rights, contact Mark Christian Subias (marksubias@earthlink.net).
HUNTER GATHERERS. © 2008 by Peter Sinn Nachtrieb. Reprinted by permission of Bruce Ostler, Bret Adams Ltd. For performance rights, contact Bruce Ostler (bostler@bretadamsltd.com)

217